ALIVE
AGAIN!

by Bill Banks

ABOUT THE AUTHOR . . .

Bill Banks attended the College of Wooster in Ohio, and then graduated from Washington University in St. Louis, Missouri with a BSBA in Business Administration. He spent eight years in the insurance business qualifying for every award offered by that industry including five times membership in the prestigious Million Dollar Round Table.

Since being healed of cancer, he and his wife, Sue, have been active in Christian publishing and book distribution, and have traveled extensively ministering and teaching with a major emphasis in the area of healing.

Alive Again!, by Bill Banks
ISBN # 0-89228-048-4
Copyright ©, 1977 Impact Books, Inc.
           now
Impact Christian Books, Inc.
332 Leffingwell Ave.,
Kirkwood, MO 63122
314-822-3309
www.impactchristianbooks.com

This book is dedicated to

LITTLE DAVEY

and all like him who need a miraculous
touch from Jesus Christ.

* * * CONTENTS * * *

A SIGHTLESS CHILD

By way of introduction to this book, I share an episode that I can barely relate today without tears; even though it happened more than seven years ago. In a way it partially explains why this book has been written.

When I was a patient in Barnes Hospital in 1970 being treated for my cancer with cobalt radiation treatments, I became aware of a child about one year old who was also undergoing radiation treatments. Little Davey (not his real name) was a sweet little guy whom the nurses were wild over. He'd had a brain tumor of some sort, had had brain surgery and had had an operation upon his eyes that had left him blind. Terrible scars ran up the side of his little head; his closed and sightless eyes made him a tragic figure that tended to haunt me. I couldn't help but compare him with my two healthy boys at home. He was only about six months younger than my Steve.

One afternoon in my room at the hospital, as I was reading my Bible the thought struck me that I should go lay my hands upon little Davey and pray for his sight to be restored. At that time I didn't know if any such thing had ever been done. I had never heard of blind eyes being healed in modern times through the laying on of hands, and besides, I told myself, "*I* have *never* laid hands upon anyone before!"

So I didn't do it. Today I would recognize the feeling that I then had, as an *anointing* to pray for someone. Since I didn't then know that God did such things, I let the enemy convince me that it was *just me!*

I wound up having my wife Sue buy a doll for me to give to little Davey. *I gave that little blind child a five dollar doll that talked, rather than a chance for his sight!* Had I been obedient to the anointing to pray for him, God

i

might just have chosen to have healed his eyes completely. I really feel that I failed God in that situation. I pray that neither I, nor anyone else, fail again in a similar situation. That's one of the reasons that I am committed to sharing God's truth concerning His healing gospel.

I certainly realize that there is "now no condemnation to them which are in Christ Jesus." (Rom. 8:1) I don't condemn myself, for we are only responsible for walking in the light that He has revealed unto us. I know that God *could have* healed Davey without me being involved. However, I also know that God is often hampered, awaiting us to do our part. We must do the *natural part* so that He can do the *supernatural part.* We create situations wherein God can move to heal people and get the glory for having done it. He needs "warm bodies": warm bodies who are willing to take Him at His word, believe His promises and step out in faith, *expecting* Him to do the miraculous part while we do the natural part!

I challenge you: Dare to believe God: dare to seek Him for what you need. He is a miracle-working God! The desire of His heart is that we seek Him, trust Him, and come to know Him well enough to know that He desires the best for us — His children whom He so greatly loves! He wants us to ask of Him, that He may do for us, that our joy might be full!

"Hitherto have ye asked nothing in my name: ask and ye shall receive, that your joy might be full." (John 16:24)

The story that follows is amazing and absolutely true. It is related as openly and as honestly as possible. Our prayer is that you will be challenged by it to press on into the wonderful world of *God's Miraculous Kingdom* and into the *Realm of the Power of the Holy Spirit!*

PART I

ALIVE AGAIN!

"I shall not die, but live and declare the works of the Lord."
(Psalm 118:17)

CHAPTER ONE.....

A DEATH SENTENCE!

"Look out, Daddy, here we come again!" "Loook . . . Oouut!

I was wrestling in the family room of my home with my two small sons who were then one and a half and three and a half. The boys were running across the room and jumping on me as I squatted near the fireplace. I'd fall over as if they'd knocked me down, and they would cackle and roll on the floor laughing. We were having a grand time, and everything was going fine until I made the mistake of thinking that the game was over before it apparently was. I looked away, and as I did my three and a half year old came running across the room wearing hard-soled shoes, and caught me with a good kick that sent me sprawling in agony on the family room floor. I've been knocked down by some of the better football players in our part of the country, but I've never seen stars nor experienced pain as I did that afternoon.

Had anyone attempted to tell me at that time that the kick was the beginning of a miracle, I'd have questioned his sanity, and would probably have laughed in his face. But it's evident now, I was experiencing a miracle, because the

1

doctors told me later, that had I not had that kick and the resultant swelling from the kick, they would never have found the tumor that I had, until they had performed an autopsy.

Within a day or so, I forgot about the pain of the kick, but later noticed some soreness which I dismissed as merely being bruised tissue or something of the sort. However, about a month later while on a trip to an insurance company convention in Toronto, Canada, which I had won by sales performance, I became acutely aware of the area of the kick; experiencing great discomfort, and profuse cold-sweating. Making some obscure pretext to my wife Sue, I went over to St. Michael's Hospital in Toronto and asked to be examined. The doctors who examined me gave me a sealed letter to deliver to my "doctor back home", which I, of course, tore open and read in the hospital parking lot. As I suspected, the doctors were quite certain that my condition was a tumor, and they suggested immediate surgery because of the diagnosis. Sue and I returned to St. Louis after the convention, planning to stop over one night, pick up our two boys, and catch a plane the next day to join a group of friends in Florida. I was still sweating and rather weak, but determined to give the family a good *last* vacation. However, that night as I tried to lift one of the suitcases, a searing flame of pain shot up through the right side of my groin.

The next morning I selected a specialist with a pleasant sounding name, and called his office for an appointment. I went to the specialist's office and after a relatively brief wait, was ushered into an examining room. The specialist came in, examined me and without a word jumped up and hurried out of the room. Now I had never been to a specialist before, and I thought perhaps they treated everyone this same way (although down deep I doubted it). He returned a few minutes later, to tell me that what

2

I had was indubitably a tumor, and although he hoped it wasn't, the nature of it indicated that it was probably malignant. He had tears in his eyes as he confirmed both my suspicions and the Canadian diagnosis. The tears began rolling down his cheeks as he said, "It's now two o'clock, I want you in Barnes Hospital by four o'clock this afternoon!"

To be perfectly frank, when your physician has tears in his eyes as he gives you his diagnosis, it doesn't inspire much optimism. So I asked, "How bad is it?"

He replied, "In cases like yours, there are only two alternatives: critical or grave. I hope we can say yours is only grave."

I was rather surprised when I found myself attempting to comfort him, saying, "It's alright. It's alright. I've had a good life and I've got no complaints, just do for me what you can."

It was at this point that I realized that I had fully 'bought' the concept of salvation. My eight years in the insurance business and some familiarity with cancer mortality tables, added to what the doctor was telling me, made it clear that my condition was terminal. Even though I had never heard of anyone 'making it' with the type of cancer that I had, I found that I wasn't concerned for myself at all. I knew that I was going home to be with the Lord. I knew that since Jesus was no respecter of persons, His promise to the penitent thief upon the cross was equally valid for me as a child of His:

"Today shalt thou be with me in Paradise!" (Luke 23:43)

As a lifelong Presbyterian — even attending the Presbyterian College of Wooster, I'd never really heard much about the subject of salvation; the subject, perhaps, being taken too much for granted, if not considered out-moded.

3

Like many another person, I'd had rather unfavorable experiences with those espousing the subject. I had been accosted coming out of the old Fox Movie Theater in St. Louis by shabbily dressed individuals, whom I'd taken at the time to be 'winos'. They would grab the lapels of their victims, and shout hungrily into their faces, "Are you saved, brother?"

I never paid any real attention to their question due to the method of their approach. But then a few years later a man at a CBMCI* dinner meeting, asked me the same question, without grabbing my lapels, or 'wrinkling my fabric'. He did it with the light of Jesus' love in his eyes. For the first time, I couldn't laugh off the question, and had to face it squarely. I mumbled a feeble, "I hope so." and began easing toward the exit.

I was able to evade the questioner but not the question; it kept rattling around in my head for days until I finally called and made an appointment with Dr. Kenneth Miller, a Presbyterian minister whom I respected greatly. I explained my dilemma to him and then asked him my question, "Am I saved?"

He explained salvation in good Presbyterian terms which I could grasp, and after further prayer and thought, I recommitted my life to Jesus Christ as Lord and SAVIOR (and never really had to worry again). Thus now, when death was imminent, I really had no fear.

I truly praise God for all the people that He in His wisdom sent across my path throughout my life; especially good Christian parents, Sunday school teachers, ministers and whoever else may have played a part in my completely accepting God's promise of salvation and eternal life. Because I can say in all honesty, that at that point and all

*Christian Business Men's Committee International — an organization with a strong evangelical Baptist flavor whose purpose is to take the gospel of salvation to businessmen.)

throughout the long months in the hospital and later in recuperating, I never doubted the fact of my salvation and it gave me great peace and comfort. I might mention that I went into the hospital fully expecting I would never come out. I expected to die a merciful death during the operation.

As I headed for home, the tears suddenly began stinging my eyes, and I knew that I wasn't ready to face Sue and the boys. I turned off the highway and drove to my parents' home. I told Mom that I had just gotten some bad news that I wanted to tell her about.

I blurted it out, "Mom, I've just come from the doctor's office; I've got cancer. They're going to operate, but it's terminal. I don't mind so much, but for the boys. They're so young!" and the tears began to flow.

Tears started down Mom's cheeks too, but she quickly countered with "It's probably not really that bad. I think maybe the Lord's going to do something good through this." Those were to be the last tears that I shed for myself, or my sorrows.

As I drove to my house I vowed to myself that neither Sue nor anyone else would be depressed by me. I was going to face it and do my best to enjoy what time I had left, wherever I had to spend it. When I got home I wrote some rather hastily scrawled notes for Sue and left them in the fireproof box we kept at home for important papers. The notes told her where my insurance policies were, and who she should contact for various types of assistance, and I even gave her a couple of suggestions as to whom she might try to sell my insurance agency.

After I wrote the notes, I went downstairs and told Sue that I had to have a little 'cyst' removed. I was admitted that afternoon to Barnes Hospital where they performed tests upon me for a couple of days. The following Monday morning they operated and removed the tumor which,

5

upon testing, did prove to be malignant. (The date that Monday was August third, 1970, my younger brother John's birthday. I later wise-cracked that although it was John's birthday, I received the birthday 'whacks'.)

After the operation the surgeon met my wife for the first time outside the operating room, and introduced her to the almost unbelievable year that was to follow with three cryptic phrases: "It was a tumor. It was malignant. If you're not worrying . . . start!" And of course she did!

I remember awakening in the recovery room after the operation. I opened my eyes and glanced around me. I was in a room filled with other hospital rolling stretchers, with unconscious people lying on them. I realized also that they had some kind of a rubber breathing tube gadget stuck down my throat which began to gag me as soon as I realized that it was there. I reached up and pushed it out of my mouth and a nurse noticed my movement and came over to my side. I asked her, "What time is it and do you have a phone in here?"

I guess she thought I was still groggy, but I wanted to call Sue and my family and tell them that I was okay — to prevent their worrying any longer.

A day or so later the team of doctors came back to me with two recommendations for treatment. They suggested first a "prophylactic operation" and to then follow that up with a maximum dosage of cobalt treatments. I found out that prophylactic surgery is 'preventative surgery'. Their plan was to split me open like the proverbial "Christmas goose" — splitting me from the breast bone straight down my trunk as far as they could go: opening me up from the front and pulling out all my organs and intestines for an "exploratory" and at the same time, to go in to my backbone and remove the lymph nodes and lymph canals up either side of the spine from the lungs downward. The first operation was a snap — this one was a "lulu!"

CHAPTER TWO.....

A FIRST GLIMPSE
OF
MIRACLE MINISTRY

When I was scheduled for the second operation nine days later, it was sufficiently serious that they gave Sue a room in Queeny Towers, a building in the Barnes Hospital complex, so that she could stay there around the clock. It was provided because of the severity of the operation and in order that she could pay the around the clock private nurses as they completed their 8 hour shifts. Sue ate her meals in the hospital restaurant for 45 days. She related to me later that they would always seat her off in a corner by herself as she was always crying or looking as if she might. However one day the *maitre de* asked her if she would mind sharing a table with someone else. This was the only time in all the months that she would eat in that restaurant, that she was ever asked to sit with someone else . . . She agreed, and was seated with a woman whom she later described to me as "one of those people whom I knew that I had never seen before, but had the instantaneous feeling that we'd met before and had known each other all our lives."

Sue said that in about three minutes they both had their life's stories out and were sharing and commiserating about me and the person that the lady had come to visit. The lady mentioned to Sue, that she had a niece in North Carolina who had also been afflicted with cancer. The niece had had both breasts removed, had cancer throughout her blood stream, and had a liver swollen up to the size of a football. She had heard of a man named Tommy Lewis who headed a mission in Kinston, North Carolina and had gone to visit him. He had prayed for her and the liver shrunk back to normal size, and within thirty days her blood stream was completely free of cancer cells. When Sue also learned that this had taken place more than six years earlier, and that the healing had lasted, she expressed interest. This kind lady offered to write her niece for the man's exact name and address.

A few days later we received a beautiful letter from the young lady recounting her story, information about Tommy Lewis and his address, and an offer to stay in her home if we were ever to come to N.C. Sue showed me the letter and then promptly put it away and pretty well forgot about it, for the time being. She later said that she had placed it in her "if I'm ever *really* desperate file", because missions and "faith healers" didn't fit into our nice, neat Presbyterian theology.

Sue told me later that after my big operation she felt that she had to kneel and pray for my healing. She admits that kneeling isn't the normal prayer position for a Methodist-turned-Presbyterian, but she was desperate and really wanted to 'get through' to God. However, she said, a very strange thing happened when she reached the privacy of her room and knelt to pray for my healing. She found that all she could do was to confess sins. The strange thing to her was that the things which she was confessing as sins were things that she didn't *intellectually* consider to be sins, such as smoking and the like.

She experienced a *presence* in the room with her. She

8

said later that she felt as though she'd had a bath from the inside out. When she stood to her feet, she was a Bible-believing Christian, fully able to accept the Divinity of Jesus Christ for the first time in her life. In the past she had been involved with the cults and the occult: fortune-tellers, horoscopes, mediums, and ouija boards.

* * * * * * *

As you may know, the recurring theme of the theology of the cults is that Jesus was not really the Son of God. They espouse that He was merely a good man, or perhaps even a great man. Christian Science, for example, calls Him the Great Gallilean Prophet, and the Way Show-er, the Great Example . . . but He wasn't the Son of God any more than you and I are sons of God.

Simple logic won't let us settle for that, if we are honest. What they have said cannot be true! Because Jesus Christ could not have been *just a good man*. They cannot have Him on their terms! Either Jesus Christ was indeed the Son of God, as *He said* that He was, or He was a *liar!* What's even worse, He must also then have been a madman, because He *believed* that He was the Son of God! Thus, we must come to the inescapable conclusion, that Jesus Christ was *everything* that He Himself said that He was, and that God the Father, through the mouths of the prophets, said He was from the beginning . . .or He was nothing!

* * * * * * *

Fortunately for me, when I was admitted to the hospital Sue was given a copy of Kathryn Kuhlman's book *I Believe In Miracles* which she literally devoured. This book started her thinking about the possibility of divine healing for me and caused her to attend a service conducted by Miss Kuhlman in St. Louis in August of 1970, just shortly after my first operation. Sue was astounded and amazed by what she saw take place at that service. She related to me later in my hospital room how she had joined some 5000 people in the Khorassan room of the Chase Hotel, in rejoicing as people by the dozens and perhaps hundreds were healed of almost every imaginable disease and condition. She was positively glowing with hope and excitement as she related the details. She said that as soon as I was able to travel we'd have to go to one of her services. I was doubtful that the people had really been healed, but Sue's enthusiasm was infectious, and I was certainly curious as to what had gotten through to her. However as it worked out, the Lord had a preliminary adventure and trip prepared for us before we'd get to see Kathryn Kuhlman.

Upon completion of the round of 25 cobalt treatments, they gave me a few weeks at home to attempt to regain my strength, and to try to get to the point where I could keep food down, and then they summoned me for more X-rays. It was at this point (about Mid-October) that they discovered a second tumor, this one located in my left lung. This news came as quite a jolt to us, since the doctors had assured us that the cancer had not spread from the original tumor site. They'd also indicated that once the lymph canals were removed, it would be impossible for any such cells to spread as the lymph canal route was the only means available for this particular type of cancer to spread. They attempted to explain away this new tumor as the result of a "stray" or "wild" cell, that had somehow gotten into the blood stream. But then they were also quick to point out, that if there were one "wild" cell, there were probably many, many more. Since this one tumor had already grown in my lung, they said I could expect more tumors to begin growing rapidly like *'clusters of grapes'* in

10

my lungs. Thus, they recommended a new series of 25 or more additional cobalt and beta-tron treatments.

The new tumor was "the straw that broke the camel's back" for Sue, and made her desperate enough to dig out the letter with Tommy Lewis' address and to write him. He called us back a few days later telling us that the time Sue had indicated as possible for us to go, would also be convenient for him, catching him between trips. So we set out for Kinston, N.C. and Tommy's Vernon Hall Mission with Sue literally dragging me around the country to get me healed. *Praise the Lord for stubborn wives.*

CHAPTER THREE.....

GOD'S SIGNPOSTS:
GOD BEHIND THE SCENES

There was an even more irresistible force in operation upon me than a stubborn wife: God Himself was working. I hadn't realized how much groundwork He had laid, until He showed me in a most unusual way, and let me know through a beautiful experience that He was indeed in charge of my situation!

When I awoke from the operations and realized that I was still alive, it both amazed me and built my faith. Since I had assumed that God *wanted me to die,* I naturally felt that the most logical time for Him to have taken me was during one of the operations. The fact that *He didn't take me, when it would have been so easy for Him, planted within my mind the possibility that maybe He didn't want me to die!*

God has promised to confirm His Word out of the mouths of two witnesses, and He will often give two witnesses to His truth for us. A few days later He used a particular Scripture to confirm for me this truth that I'd sensed.

"What profit is there in my blood, when I go down to the pit? Shall the dust praise thee? shall it declare thy truth?" (Psalm 30:9)

A. THE MYSTERY OF THE "BEES"

I share two stories, two signposts, wherein I did not at the time perceive what I now feel God was trying to show me; in order that others might profit from my lack of understanding. Now, I feel that if I had then realized that the Lord was trying to show me that He *did* intend to heal me, it would have both built my faith and hastened my healing. He was endeavoring to give me an indication — through my circumstances — of His will. At that time I did not sufficiently know His Word, and was not then seeking His will through His Word — His will to heal me!

* * * * * * *

It is strange that I would recall the dream, in that I rarely dream or if I do, I rarely, if ever, recall dreaming. The nightmares that I have had in a lifetime, you could count upon one hand.

As a little child I did have a horrible recurring nightmare. I was raised in a wonderful, loving Christian home, was blessed with loving parents and family and had no special problems, nor traumas in my life, . . . no real fears that I can recall. However, I did have one particular recurring nightmare. The nightmare came to me in stages, because I was unable to take it all at one time. It must have first come to me when I was about four years old. It was so unbelievably frightening to me, that the indescribably intense fear (and later actual sensations of intense pain) would awaken me each time before the dream could unfold or progress very far.

It always began the same way; I would become aware of being immersed or enveloped in the blackest blackness I'd ever seen, as if I were looking at black velvet in pitch black darkness . . . and then, the pain would begin. There would be an almost indescribable pain in the center of my stomach at about or slightly below the belt line, as if someone had a huge, pointed fence-post-like stake in my navel; and as if they were leaping up and down upon it.

I would awaken screaming in fright and with an actual sensation of pain. My mother would come in and ask me to tell her what the problem was and then what the dream was like, and I was unable to even talk about it, apparently because of the almost paralyzing fear.

Each succeeding time the nightmare would reoccur, I would manage to remain in the dream a little bit longer before the panic would awaken me.

The next stage that this nightmare took, was to have me seem to wake up. As I opened my eyes I saw a scene that caused my fear to accelerate till I thought my heart would burst. I was in a bright, clean room lying in a prone position facing upward into brilliant light and I was surrounded by greenish colored *"bees!"* I could hear them buzzing in a muted fashion but what was really terrifying to me was the fact that they appeared to be *eating me!* Although I was for some reason unable to see my stomach, I felt as if they were all, with great intensity and concentration, devouring me.

My logical, analytical mind came into play even at that early age, and even in the semi- or unconscious dream state, I began to analyse the situation and to ask myself questions:

"Why did these "bees" hate me so much that they wanted to eat me?"

"Why were these "bees" green in color?" All I had ever seen were yellow, or black and yellow."

The next installment of the dream added some new details. I again awakened looking into the same brightness, and then again realized that I was surrounded by the green "bees." I tried hard to scream, but I couldn't get any

15

sound to emerge from my throat. Fortunately they seemed to take no notice of my having awakened. I could see the "bees" focusing with apparent relish upon my mid-section, at the site of my intense, pulsating, throbbing pain. I could also hear their seemingly excited, yet droning buzzing.

The final installment provided still additional puzzle pieces. As I tried unsuccessfully to scream, one of the "bees", the one closest to me on my right, turned away from the feast, from which he seemed a bit aloof, and moved over, closer to my head. My heart leaped again with fear, as I thought he was going to begin to eat my face, but then I sensed his compassion, and I noticed his eyes. As this "bee" looked at me, his blue eyes were filled with compassion and I noticed he was wearing gold-rimmed spectacles similar to the style my father had worn when I was a little child. (Now they're called "Granny-glasses".) Somehow, crazy as it sounded, he seemed to be familiar to me. And then, wonder of wonders, he spoke to me, "It's all right, Bill. It's alright, just relax, we'll be through in a minute." And then from my left, I heard a soft, female voice echo, "It's alright. It's alright, just relax."

I closed my eyes with an inaudible sigh of relief on my lips. I felt the dream was now complete and the fear was gone: they apparently didn't hate me after all! I fell asleep and slept peacefully through the night. Weeks later for the first time, I was finally able to jokingly discuss with my mother the horrible recurring dream I'd had so often.

But there were still several lingering, perplexing questions hanging around in my mind for which I had no answers:

- "Why was there compassion in the eyes of the friendly 'bee'?"
- "Why did that 'bee' have blue eyes?"
- "Why did the male 'bee's' voice seem vaguely familiar to me?"

- "Why did the 'bees' speak in English? and/or how could I understand the bees (or at least some of them; the rest seemed only to buzz)?
- "How did they know my name?"
- "Why did the one 'bee' wear gold-rimmed glasses?"
- "Why was there a female 'bee'?"

I had long since filed the dream away, as just a nutty nightmare. I had completely forgotten about it.

B. THE SOLUTION THIRTY YEARS LATER.

During the second, big operation, a heavy-set male anethesist inserted a needle into my left arm and said, "Just take a few deep breaths."

Attempting to lighten the mood, I wise-cracked, "You aren't going to give me that old 'count backwards from 100 routine,' like in the movies are you?"

With a condescending smirk, he said, "I don't think we'll need that."

Pow! I was gone . . . floating gently into blackness. The total deep blackness that people usually seem to experience when anesthesised.

Suddenly something clicked in my mind and I became instantly alert: I was acutely aware of the blackness, a *deep velvety blackness* that was somehow familiar . . . It was the same blackness that I had seen in my childhood dream . . . and then the same terrible panic struck me as I felt the jabbing, pulsating pain once again, of the bouncing stake in my navel!

My attention was momentarily distracted from my pain and panic, as a circle of clear light similar to a bright moon in appearance appeared directly before my still closed eyes. "Hmm," I mused, "that is my 'sphere of consciousness'."

17

After a few moments of observation, I realized that the sphere had begun to rapidly shrink and was floating upwards and off to my right. It continued shrinking until it was about the size of a pea, and then I heard myself exclaim, "My sphere of consciousness is shrinking . . . *I'm dying!*" After another moment, I announced to myself, "It won't be long, now!"

Whummmp! A sharp blow struck my chest. It was followed a few seconds later with another hard Whummmp! accompanied by a, "Come on Bill! Come on Bill!"

I opened my eyes and looked straight up into a bright light about two and a half feet across, reminiscent of those I'd seen in dentists' offices.

I realized that just as in my earliest dream, I was trying with all my might to scream, but no sounds were coming out of my mouth — due to the suction tubes, and breathing apparatus down my throat.

I was afraid to move my eyes because I could hear the familiar buzzing of my old enemies . . . the bees! I looked down toward the source of my pain, but my view was partially blocked by a surgical sheet projecting 8 inches or so above my chest, preventing me from seeing my chest and stomach area.

However, to my amazement, I was surrounded by 'green bees'! But in spite of the buzzing, they weren't bees at all . . . they were the surgical team dressed not only in their green gowns which I had seen before, but also in green surgical *caps and masks* which they had not worn before I was "knocked out". The only human portion of them now visible to my gaze was their eyes. The buzzing was actually there, but it was the indistinguishable sounds of eight or so voices, all muttering to one another at the same time.

Waves of relief began flowing through my mind. Then the figure closest to me on my right, turned to face me and

I *did* recognize him. He looked at me with compassionate blue eyes, rimmed with gold 'granny glasses', and said, "It's all right, Bill. It's all right."

Then, from my left a familiar, soft female voice, with a pat upon my arm said "It's alright. It's alright. Just relax. Take a few deep breaths and you'll go back to sleep."

Before I slipped off again, the realization came . . . the reason that the friendly 'bee' had seemed familiar to me, was that he was a young doctor whom I had met and insured about four years before the operation. Of course, in my earliest dreams, I couldn't have recognized him, even had I seen his full face, as the dream predated my meeting him by more than twenty years!

The day after the operation, I told Sue that I had something to tell her, but that I wouldn't be able to discuss it with her for days. The experience was still too fresh and painful to even put into words for nearly a week. Finally though, I shared with her and later with my family the story of the fantastic fulfillment of my dream in exact detail, during the operation.

After sharing it with a resident from another hospital, he told me that he felt that if I had indeed awakened on the operating table, that no one would ever admit it because I might have grounds for a lawsuit against the anesthesist. Thus forewarned, I waited for an opportunity to catch my friend, the young doctor, alone so I could verify my experience. Each time I saw him for the next week, he was accompanied by interns. Finally one afternoon, my opportunity came, and I cautiously began testing, "Sandy, do you ever wear gold-rimmed glasses?"

He looked startled and said, "How did you know?" I do wear a pair of gold rimmed glasses, but I only wear them in the operating room!"

He pulled a red case out of his pocket and opened it to show me the glasses, I now knew only too well.

19

I continued my cautious attack for truth, "I woke up on the operating table and I saw you wearing them during my second operation."

"Naw, you didn't wake up, you imagined it. People often dream while they're under anesthetic."

"Sandy," I insisted, "I woke up after being thumped on the chest twice and I can tell you exactly what happened: You were standing off to my right. You came over to me, wearing your glasses and you said, "It's alright. It's alright.""

"Oh yeah, I remember now: I happened to be free and dropped in to observe your operation. (The reason that he seemed aloof from the proceedings.) You did come to. It rarely occurs and when it does people usually can't remember it afterwards."

"Something else, Sandy, after you spoke to me, I heard a woman's voice repeat almost the same thing that you had said."

"Sure," he explained, "That was Mary, the woman who administered the anesthesia to you."

"But," I interrupted, "a woman didn't put me to sleep, it was a heavy-set fellow who wore glasses."

"By Golly, you're right! I remember now; he did start the operation, but he got called out about 15 minutes after the operation started to help on an emergency case, and Mary came in to relieve him. You really were alert!"

I don't pretend to fully understand why I had the dream, but I know that when I awoke on the operating table my reaction was one of tremendous relief. I was overjoyed that I wasn't being eaten by bees; rather than shocked or filled with fear that could perhaps have killed me. Also there was within me a tremendously deep awareness that God had been preparing me for something for a long time; a feeling of rejoicing that was now as strong as the earlier fear had been.

Almost a month later the Lord showed me something

else about my dream that staggered me with even more love, admiration, and awe for Him. He guided me to read in the Book of Psalms and I began reading Psalm 118:

"It is <u>better</u> <u>to</u> <u>trust</u> <u>in</u> <u>the</u> <u>Lord</u> than to put confidence in man.
It is better to trust in the Lord than to put confidence in princes.
All nations compassed me about: but in the name of the Lord will I destroy them.
They compassed me about; yea, they compassed me about: but in the name of the Lord I will destroy them.

My heart began racing with anticipation; I came to the 12th verse and I gasped when I read:

They compassed me about <u>like</u> <u>bees</u>; they are quenched as the fire of thorns: for in the name of the Lord I will destroy them.
Thou has thrust sore at me that I might fall: but <u>the</u> <u>Lord</u> <u>helped</u> <u>me.</u>
<u>The</u> <u>Lord</u> is <u>my</u> <u>strength</u> <u>and</u> <u>song</u>, <u>and</u> <u>is</u> <u>become</u> <u>my</u> <u>salvation</u>.
The voice of rejoicing and salvation is in the tabernacles of the righteous: the right hand of the Lord doeth valiantly. <u>The</u> <u>right</u> <u>hand</u>* <u>of</u> <u>the</u> <u>Lord</u> <u>is</u> <u>exalted</u>: the right hand of the Lord doeth valiantly.
<u>I</u> <u>shall</u> <u>not</u> <u>die</u>, <u>but</u> <u>live</u>, <u>and</u> <u>declare</u> <u>the</u> <u>works</u> <u>of</u> <u>the</u> <u>Lord</u>. The Lord hath chastened me sore: but <u>He</u> <u>hath</u> <u>not</u> <u>given</u> <u>me</u> <u>over</u> <u>unto</u> <u>death.</u>
Open to me the gates of righteousness: I will go into them, and I will praise the Lord.
This gate of the Lord, into which the righteous shall enter, <u>I</u> <u>will</u> <u>praise</u> <u>thee</u>: <u>for</u> <u>thou</u> <u>has</u> <u>heard</u> <u>me</u>, and art become my salvation.
The stone which the builders refused is become the head stone of the corner.
<u>This</u> <u>is</u> <u>the</u> <u>Lord's</u> <u>doing</u>; <u>it</u> <u>is</u> <u>marvelous</u> <u>in</u> <u>our</u> <u>eyes.</u>

*Jesus Christ is *the right hand of the Lord.*

The Psalm seemed to perfectly summarize my dream and my new life. They (God's enemies and my enemies) indeed tried to *destroy me;* but by His grace and power I was delivered and I shall defeat His enemies by means of *His strength.* I continue to seek to *exalt the right hand of the Lord* because He has let me *not die, but live* and I *shall praise Him* and *declare His works!*

I share this with you to show how God can speak to us through our *circumstances.* Even as Joseph said to his brothers when they met him in Egypt, "You intended it for evil, but *God intended it for good."*

Even though Satan had taken his worst shot at me, God was still able to protect and keep that which was entrusted to Him. Had I been as discerning as I should have been, I would no doubt have seen in these circumstances or "coincidences", manifest evidence of God's hand intervening in my situation. I should have been able to enter into His rest, and ceased from my own concerns and worries.

Very often along the pathway of our journey toward healing, God does give us little "love gifts"; *sign posts* of his love pointing us toward the ultimate victory which He has intended for us. These *sign posts*, or love gifts are things that God graciously sends into our lives, perhaps a person, a thing, a tangible gift, some action performed for us or that we observe, some unexpected plus, some blessing along the way that reminds us *of the love of God for us.* They function as a personal indication to us of His love; they are reminders of His love. Just as flowers on a birthday serve as a reminder or token of someone's love for you, so do these sign posts serve, as reminders of the great love they represent, and of the great power working in our behalf . . . and they bespeak themselves of that future victory . . . that healing, or whatever it may be that we are trusting God to accomplish for us.

C. THE SIGN OF THE CHAIR

Another very strange and yet beautiful thing happened to me just after the big operation.

A few nights after this operation, the doctors felt that I could be permitted to begin moving, at least to the point of being able to walk to the bathroom if someone was there to assist me.

I share this incident especially because I didn't appreciate its significance at the time it occurred, and perhaps if you're also seeking a miracle, you may be able to learn from my having lacked perception. In retrospect, I firmly believe that God was trying even then to let me know that He was in control of my situation, and gave this sign as an indication of his desire to heal me.

Late one night, my roommate was asleep, the lights were out and it was probably about midnight. I felt that I needed to visit the bathroom. I buzzed my buzzer and was unable to get anyone to answer. Since no one had arrived to help me, and being a little stubborn and overly self-sufficient anyway, I decided to try it on my own.

I got to my feet rather feebly and managed to make my way to the bathroom by supporting myself upon the metal foot of my bed and then the metal foot of my roommate's bed. Once there, I found that I really didn't need to be there after all, and began to feel really dizzy. I rang repeatedly for the nurse again, on the buzzer system in the bathroom, but still to no avail. After ten or fifteen minutes, of watching the bathroom walls flip everytime my heart would beat, I determined to try to make my way back to my bed without their help as I didn't want to die in that bathroom.

I was able to pull myself to my feet with the aid of the bar on the wall for that purpose. I got through the door supporting myself upon the wall and the handle of the

23

door, and then I started across the room. I lurched to the relative security of a handgrip upon the foot of my roommate's bed (a distance of perhaps 4 feet) and then I attempted to reach the foot of my own bed (another distance of perhaps 4 feet). After taking the first faltering step, or perhaps as soon as I released my handhold, I knew that I wasn't going to be able to make it . . . I knew I was going to fall!

That realization sent a feeling of numbed panic into the pit of my stomach. I knew that the incision, running nearly the full length of my torso, hadn't even had the stitches removed from it yet. I knew that I would surely pop, like an overripe melon, upon hitting the floor or any intervening furniture.

Then it was if those concerns melted, and I heard myself observe in my mind, "Well it doesn't matter any longer. I can't do anything about it, anyway. Here I go . . . ."

Suddenly, time seemed to stop for me, and I felt as if I had floated down into a ball of cotton. I realized that I was down and there hadn't been so much as a flicker of pain! I had fallen across the guest chair footstool, which had caught me just above the lap, supporting my torso to the middle of my chest. The upper portion of my torso landed in the seat of the guest chair itself. I wasn't hurt in the slightest! My face felt as if it were buried in cotton rather than deeply into the seat of the overstuffed chair. I found that I was totally helpless, however. I hadn't the strength with which to pull myself up or even to move my arms.

After a period of perhaps another five or ten minutes, a nurse came in carrying a flashlight and asked, "What are you doing, Mr. Banks? Did you get dizzy?"

I fought back the urge to make a reply like, "No, I just

wanted to study this chair a bit more closely." and instead simply said, "Yes."

I could so easily have been badly injured in that fall: six inches either way, and I'd have hit the arm of the chair. God was protecting and trying to get through to me that He was in control!

In the months that were to follow I would need to know God's presence. I could not have even guessed at the exciting and terrifying experiences that lay ahead.

CHAPTER FOUR.....

THE QUEST BEGINS

Just shortly before our plane landed in Kinston, N.C., Sue who'd been reading in her Bible, leaned over to share a passage with me that had caused her eyes to glisten. "Listen to this!" she said:

> *"Is any sick among you? Let him call for the elders of the church and let them pray over him, anointing him with oil in the name of the Lord: And the prayer of faith shall save the sick, and the Lord shall raise him up; and if he has committed sins, they shall be forgiven him.*
> *Confess your faults one to another, and pray one for another, that ye may be healed. The effectual fervent prayer of a righteous man availeth much."* James 5:14-16

Sue turned to me and said, "Wouldn't it be a beautiful thing, if we could get someone to do that for you before . . ." She was unable to finish the sentence.

I quickly agreed that it would, indeed, be a beautiful thing if we could get someone to do it for me, *before it was too late.*

After having bounced around on a local connecting flight via a small airline, we finally landed in what appeared to be an impossibly small airstrip (even for such a small plane). We went into the terminal building which was reminiscent of the airports of World War II vintage. It had one counter for everything: tickets, claims, baggage, ticket check, ticket sales etc., and on the other side of the building was a coke machine and a snack counter. Before I really had a chance to assess the airport building we were engulfed by a group of people among whom was Tommy Lewis; all the rest of the group were friends or members of his Mission who were there to catch our plane on its outbound flight.

Tommy was an interesting looking man, not in the slightest what I'd expected such a "man of God" to look like. I'd had the impression that anyone who answered his phone at home with "Praise the Lord!" rather than a simple "Hello", would glow or at least look 'holy'. However, he looked to me like a middle-aged ex-basketball player. He was tall, and lanky and was wearing a faded gray sweatshirt. My faith was not enhanced by his appearance, which also didn't help to allay in any way my concern about the nature of the Vernon Hall Mission. I found that I was beginning to share Sue's suspicion that we might be spending the night sleeping on the pews of a store front church, and was secretly thankful that for that very reason she'd insisted that I bring pajamas.

When we entered his brand new car in the parking lot, I began to have doubts about my first impression. I found a measure of peace began to return as we talked with him while he drove. As I listened to him, it became apparent to me that he was both intelligent and sincere, even if under-dressed, and more important that *He loved the Lord.*

After driving through the town, Tommy turned the car sharply to the right and we entered a long, tree-lined winding driveway and we found ourselves "face-to-face" with the Vernon Hall Mission, one of the most beautiful ante-bellum three story brick mansions that I had ever seen. I was awe struck and my analytical mind began to reel because of some of the amazing contradictions I'd seen.

28

This home could easily have come straight from the pages of *"Gone With The Wind"*.

The house was surrounded by ten acres of woods, and inside, had one of those large entrance hallways, merging into a wide staircase, that went up half a flight and then split into two flights of stairs that went up to form a second floor hallway and balcony of sorts over-looking the first floor hallway. We couldn't believe that this was the Vernon Hall Mission that we'd been worrying about. Tommy said simply, "This is our Mission."

We were ushered inside and introduced to his gentle, soft-spoken wife. Tommy and his lovely wife suggested that Sue and I go upstairs to a bedroom to clean up and rest after our journey. (I appreciated that as I was still pretty shakey from the weakness of the operations and the cobalt treatments.) They said simply, "We'll visit more after you've had a chance to rest."

About an hour later we went downstairs and a clean-shaven Tommy handed me some literature on healing to read and then left us alone. I noticed him a little while later sitting in his car with another man a little way down the driveway, apparently praying. I assumed that he was seeking guidance or strength for the healing "endeavors" to come, although I never asked him about it. A little later he came in and we sat down to dinner with his family; Tommy, his wife, and a teen-age son.

Sue couldn't restrain her curiosity, and asked Tommy's wife, almost as soon as dinner began, "How did you come to have such a lovely mission-er-home?"

The answer was fascinating. Tommy's story is a fantastic account of "how if you trust the Lord, and listen, and yield to Him . . . He will provide." Tommy experienced a "new birth" late in life; I believe he said he was in his mid-thirties when the Lord spoke to his heart for the first time in a real way. A short while later, Tommy was walking down the streets of Kinston, and the Lord spoke to him in an audible way and said something to the effect of, "I want you to go up to that house and claim it for My work."

Now I'm sure Tommy's reaction was probably like ours would have been, "*That* house, Lord? You know that is the biggest house in town." But being a yielded Christian, he did as he was told. He knocked upon the door and when it was opened to him, he said to the man standing there, "You probably won't believe this, but as I was walking down the street just now, the Lord spoke to me and told me to come up and claim this house for His work." *And would you believe it?* the man said, "I'm glad you're here. My mother died last year and the taxes on this place are eating me up, it's too big for me. Come on in, and we'll draw up the papers." *Praise the Lord* is right!

During dinner some of my "denominational hangups" began to nag me, and I felt that I had to find out what "brand" he was. So I asked if his Mission was associated with any particular denomination. He said, "No, we are completely free of any denominational ties, and support. We rely entirely upon the faith offerings of the supporters of the mission." (As I write this it may sound as if he were hinting for a donation but that is absolutely not the case. At no time while we were their guests did they ever treat us as anything other than guests, or old friends. I had the distinct feeling that we were being treated just as if we had been members of their own family.)

After dinner while Tommy was on the phone, his wife explained to us that their normal procedure was for Tommy merely to counsel with sick people, share Scriptures relating to healing with them and to then pray alone with them. However, in my case, they had "felt led" to operate a little differently. "Tommy and I both feel that we should follow the plan outlined in *James chapter five.*

(That we should summon elders, and that the elders should anoint you with oil and pray for your healing.) He and I each independently made up a list of five elders from our group that we should summon. When we put the lists together they were *identical*." Then she went on excitedly, "We have invited them and all five have agreed to come over after dinner tonight."

She also mentioned that Tommy had been fasting for several days for my healing. I was amazed that anyone would take that much interest in someone whom he really didn't even know.

Incidentally, being pretty much of a skeptic, when I heard all this about James, Chapter 5, I concluded to myself, that somehow Sue and these people were "in cahoots" and were trying to "psych me up" to get me healed!

The Lord dealt very graciously with my *honest* skepticism. That evening when the elders arrived and began talking with one another, they realized that none of them had any oil, and that there was no oil in the house with which to anoint me. So, they had to send one of the elders out to a local grocery store to get some olive oil. The Lord, very graciously, dealing with my skepticism and confirming for me that in truth, this was not their normal way of ministering to people and had obviously not been pre-arranged.

A little while after dinner we were ushered into their family room which had probably originally been a library or study. Very shortly, people began to drop in one by one, until our little group as finally comprised was about nine or ten in number, all men with the exception of my wife, Mrs. Lewis, and one very sweet lady a little older. The men, as I recall, aside from Tommy and myself, were Tommy's brother Bob, a Baptist minister, and a high school teacher.

When the elder returned from the store with the oil, Tommy then set the stage by talking a little bit about Christian healing and read again the passage from James chapter five describing the procedure. They then anointed my head with oil in the name of the Lord and began to pray for me. Just as we had expected, it was indeed a beautiful, Scriptural experience! But then they began to do something very un-Presbyterian, un-Methodist, un-anything else that I was familiar with, they began to pray "in tongues!"

I had never heard anyone pray in tongues before in my life, and I had always associated it with people frothing at the mouth, and flailing upon the floor and climbing up the walls and doing all those strange things that we have somehow been taught to believe would happen. However, none of those things happened, they merely changed languages and I couldn't understand a word that they were speaking. Perhaps the strangest thing to me was the fact that it wasn't offensive to me as I had always thought it would surely be, if ever I were to hear anyone speak in tongues. It was no more offensive, than if they had begun praying for me in German, or Hebrew, or Swahili or any other language which was unknown to me.

The group prayed calmly and seeming earnestly in their "devotional languages". Although I *knew* they had to be "psyched up" to do this, I had to admit to myself that no one in the room with the possible exception of Sue and myself appeared to be the least bit excited or emotional.

I was convinced however that God wasn't really involved in the proceedings. I felt that I had a pretty good relationship with the Lord, (how easily we become set in our prideful ways.) I *knew* that if *He* were involved, He'd *let me know!* He'd have let me hear the sound of the "mighty rushing wind", or my skin would have tingled, or my nape hair would have stood up, something — anything!

When they first laid their hands upon me and began to pray for my healing specifically, in English, as well as afterwards in tongues, I could feel that their hands were trembling. Sue later tried to convince me that they "were under the power of the Holy Spirit" and that it was His power flowing into and through them into me, that had caused their hands to shake. Now that, I really couldn't buy! I rationalized to myself that they had permitted themselves to become emotionally involved in trying to help the Lord get me healed, and in so doing they had "psyched themselves up" to the point where they were actually physically shaking.

I have since learned a beautiful definition of "faith", which I believe may have originated with Derek Prince, to the effect that "Faith is *believing* the Word of God (as contained in the Scriptures) *in spite of* what our senses tell us!"

After they had prayed what they apparently felt was a sufficient length of time for me, they turned to Sue, and asked if she'd like to receive "the Baptism in the Holy Spirit?" I was extremely surprised to hear her reply, "Sure." (She explained to me later that she had read something about it in David Wilkerson's book *The Cross And the Switchblade,* and knew then that she wanted it, if it were ever to be made available to her.)

The group then moved over to encircle her. They followed essentially the same procedure . . . laid their hands upon her . . . prayed in English, asking for the Baptism in the Holy Spirit . . . and then began praying in tongues. When they had completed their praying, I looked at Sue, and she was positively as red as an apple. Almost immediately she began complaining about 'waves of heat' flowing through her body, and actual drops of sweat were visible upon her face. The group joked about the Lord also baptizing with fire, as Mrs. Lewis went to get her a glass of iced-tea.

As a 'good skeptic' I had an explanation for this also: the combination of these people 'psyching themselves up', plus the obvious embarrassment of being the center of attention, plus the natural body heat of the group gathered around her, accounted for the warmth which she was experiencing! The Lord very graciously proved me wrong about this too, because the waves of heat lasted for four days! I can still recall Sue in the nights that followed, kicking off the covers one minute, and pulling them back over her a few minutes later.

After the group had prayed for Sue, they turned back to me and said, "Bill, would you like to receive the Baptism in the Holy Spirit?" I must confess that I really didn't have the slightest idea what they were talking about. My theology at that point, I believe, was just barely sufficient, for me to be able to grasp the concept of *water baptism,* much less a *Baptism in or with the Holy Spirit!*

Seriously though, I felt, that if it was something from God, I *wanted it* and I'd take it "ala'mode" if I could get it! (Some foolishly say that tongues or other gifts are "lesser," and they want only the best gifts. Not me! I'll take any gift God has, small or great. God only gives *good* and *perfect gifts.* Therefore everything He gives is going to be a great blessing!) So I said "Yes."

They again laid their hands upon me, and prayed, this time for me to receive the Baptism in the Holy Spirit. I made the mistake most commonly made by people being prayed for to receive the Baptism, without having received instruction as to what it is and as to what to expect. I sat there with my *teeth clenched tightly shut.* I was praying for the Lord to Baptize me, and to give me a new language if He wanted to, but I was waiting for the Lord to grab my jaws, to force them open, to wiggle my tongue, and to make strange noises to come out of my mouth.

The Lord did not, of course, do any one of those

things, and He won't! He isn't going to force us to speak in tongues! If he were going to force us, *we'd have all been speaking in tongues for a long time!*

Therefore, needless to say, I didn't speak in tongues and really didn't feel that I had received the Baptism or anything else, for that matter.

The next morning after a big breakfast, which we ate with Mrs. Lewis, as Tommy had left early to take his son to school, Tommy returned and drove us to the airport where we caught a plane for home. Our spirits were somewhat dampened as nothing really tangible happened except that we had had a beautiful Scriptural experience, and had met some beautiful people who truly believed the Bible.

On the plane, I mused over what had happened and I realized something: Although I thought that these people possessed some bad theology, I couldn't fault the 'fruit' of their Christianity. I remembered that both Jesus and Paul had spoken of Christians being known by the "fruit", borne out in their lives and actions. Based upon their fruit, I had to confess that these people were good Christians. They had welcomed us into their home, put us up over night, fed us all the appropriate number of meals, and had asked nothing of us in return . . . except for the privilege of praying for my healing! The fruit was certainly there, even if I thought that they didn't know the Bible as well as I *thought* I did, and even if I couldn't buy all of their theology.

Since I didn't think that anything had happened at Kinston, I was in no particular hurry to get back to the doctor for another X-ray. However, about three weeks later, I did have another X-ray which seemingly confirmed my suspicions, as the tumor in my left lung was still there and medically unchanged. This fact, coupled with the doctors' recommendation of a second, maximum round of cobalt treatments, this time on my left lung, prompted Sue to beg them to delay the treatments for a month. This also prompted the second jaunt in our search for the "Holy Grail" of healing.

CHAPTER FIVE.....

JESUS MOVING
IN A KATHRYN KUHLMAN MEETING?

The second jaunt in our search for healing was a trip to a Kathryn Kuhlman meeting in Pittsburgh, Pennsylvania. Kathryn Kuhlman became a lot more widely known afterwards, but at that time in November of 1970 I had never heard of her until Sue had been given the copy of *I Believe in Miracles*.

Sue appeared to be bent upon driving me crazy with two things while I was 'trying to quietly die of cancer': Kathryn Kuhlman on television and Derek Prince tapes. Sue seemed to be convinced that if she could just get me to watch enough of Kathryn Kuhlman on television I would somehow manage to absorb a healing. I couldn't take Miss Kuhlman on television. I didn't believe anyone could really be like she appeared to be on T.V., so sanguinely, and sugary sweet, and even her overly dramatic and somewhat gravelly voice seemed to irritate me. Having afterwards been in her services, and even had opportunities to usher in her services, I learned to truly love the woman, and know that she was mightily used of God, and surely was His "handmaiden!" But at that time, I couldn't stand to watch her, I'd have to leave the room when she came on T.V. or immediately go to sleep.

Some measure of faith upon my part may have been involved in the trip to Pittsburgh, as Satan really fought our making the trip. (As he always does when God is about to open a door.) I was somewhat apprehensive about being able to make the trip from the outset, as I was still being troubled with the side effects of the cobalt, nausea and diarrhea and so weak I hadn't been able to stand for more than about five minutes at a time.

To make matters even worse, two hours before we were to leave for the airport, I became violently sick to my stomach. I was sicker than I had ever been before in my life!

SUE'S VISION

Realizing how sick and weak I was, and not being totally sure whether it was God or Satan trying to prevent our making the trip, Sue decided to seek the Lord's guidance. She prayed, "Lord, I'm going to close my eyes, and if *you* want us to go this afternoon, let me see a green light; if not, let me see a red one."

When she closed her eyes, she saw neither light, but rather saw something that she will never forget. While she prayed, God gave her a vision of the crucifixion. She saw Jesus upon the cross, in a way she had never seen portrayed in statues, paintings or films. The agony of His suffering during the three hours of darkness was indescribable, and she was startled and overwhelmed by the amount of blood that He shed. As the picture faded from her mind's eye, she heard herself crying over and over, "I'm sorry!" "I'm sorry!" in realization that His agony had been

38

for her sins and faults. As the experience finished, she instinctively arose and began packing for our trip to Pittsburgh. It was as though the Lord were showing her that HE had died *for my healing* as well as her sins. In fact, later in the day reflecting upon my sickness, the Lord said gently to her, "For this I died!"

Beautifully enough, as Sue started packing, my strength began to return at least to the degree that I could walk.

We flew out to Pittsburgh and the following morning went to the Presbyterian Church where the Kuhlman Services were held. We were careful to arrive by 5:45 a.m., as we had been warned to get there before 6:00 a.m., in order to have a chance at a seat. The sky was pitch black when we arrived at the church, but there was already a group of perhaps one hundred people huddled together on the front steps of the church. They were huddled together for warmth and to protect one another from the bone-chilling wind. The scene was eerily illuminated by the light from a multi-storied Christmas tree, formed of strings of white lights, at Macy's department store on the opposite side of the street, diagonally down the block.

A few minutes after we arrived, a gentle snow began. As I stood there in the line until nine o'clock, when the doors were opened, more than once I asked myself, "What are you doing here?" However, the optimism and expectancy of the crowd was infectious and accounts of personally witnessed miracles in previous services were rampant and encouraging.

I amazed Sue, not to mention myself, by being able to remain on my feet during the wait even though I had several periods of nausea, cold-sweating, dizziness, and nearly fainted a time or two. Promptly at nine o'clock the doors were opened and somehow, we managed to get inside the church and obtained pretty good seats. Although the church seated probably nine hundred to a thousand, nearly the same number remained outside when it was full. (One year later I took some relatives to a similar service, and although I got them in, I was unable to get in myself. God had gotten me in when I needed to be there!)

Once inside, after a brief wait they sang a hymn and the service was under way. Suddenly she was on stage, and you could almost feel the charged atmosphere of expectancy as she led the group in the singing of "How Great Thou Art." Her deep, scratchy voice seemed pleasing and even awe-inspiring in the context of the service. My petty prejudice against women in the pulpit in her case vanished, as I clearly saw her to be God's instrument.

Without any preliminaries, it seemed, she began calling out the "healings". She boomed out, "There's been ears opened in the balcony. . . High blood-pressure healed up there too, . . . heart trouble's gone . . . and now down here on the main floor . . . diabetes healed . . . speech defect healed . . . " and on and on, for about five minutes.

I sat there like any good skeptic might, thinking to myself, "Anybody can *say* these things." Once again, the Lord proved me wrong, as He had in Kinston. The people started trooping down the aisles to a microphone, to relate how the Lord had healed them while she was speaking. Some testified that they had felt heat flow through their bodies, some had felt cool, some a tingle of electricity, some had felt nothing at all, but merely noticed the absence of their symptoms. (It is important to note: the Lord works in a great variety of ways to administer His healing power. We err if we attempt to put Him in a box by expecting something to happen in a particular way. We must recognize His sovereignty, and *let Him* be God!)

The first fellow to reach the microphone, fairly shouted, "Praise the Lord, I've just been healed of diabetes!" My natural reaction was, "How on earth would he know? Even if he *had been healed* of his diabetes, he isn't a doctor, and he obviously hasn't had time to get to a doctor to be checked or tested. Certainly, he has merely 'psyched himself up' to the point that since she mentioned a healing of diabetes, he has convinced himself that he's been healed; but he is merely deluded!"

I remained skeptical throughout the first half or two-thirds of the service, until I saw a little eight year old boy standing up there, with tears streaming down his cheeks. His parents standing behind him with tears streaming down their cheeks, praising God and giving glory to Jesus Christ because the Lord had opened his ear in that service. He was hearing out of it for the first time in his life. Kathryn had him face away from her so that he couldn't read her lips and repeat everything that she said, which he did perfectly! I knew that the best actors in Hollywood could not have faked the scene that I had just witnessed!

Shortly after the little boy was healed, Sue thrust an elbow into my side and whispered loudly, "Are you praying for your healing?" I quickly changed the subject and sloughed off her question, as I had always done in the past. The reason I was uncomfortable with that question was due to my "theology."

* * * * * * *

My thinking at that point went something like this: "If God hadn't wanted me to die of cancer, *He* wouldn't have given me the cancer in the first place. Therefore, how could I as a mere mortal, with mortal intelligence, try to tell an omniscient, all-knowing God that He had made a mistake in my case, or try to change His mind in my case? You see, I thought I knew what God's will for my life was: that being to die of cancer!"

I couldn't pray through the "steel shield" over my head of "Thy will be done." I assumed that God's will for me

41

was to die of cancer. My prayers went like this: "Lord I know that your word states that before I can phrase the needs of my heart into a prayer, to ask you to heal me, to not leave my two children under five fatherless . . . that you know that prayer before I can utter it. However, *if it is your will* for me to die at this early age, I accept it, 'Thy will be done'!"

You see, I couldn't pray through that steel shield. This problem, like most of our spiritual problems, stem from our either misquoting or not understanding God's word. In this case it is a matter of taking God's Word out of context. It should read, *"Thy will be done on earth,"* (comma not period) *"as it is in Heaven."* (Mt. 6:10) In Heaven there is no cancer, no pain, no suffering, no death!

I didn't realize then that *God's perfect will for us* was accomplished two thousand years ago upon Calvary's Cross when Jesus paid the full price, not just for sin and *salvation* . . . but also for sickness and *health!**

"He Himself bore our sicknesses and our infirmities." Mt. 8:17

* * * * * * *

God was to use this experience in Pittsburgh to touch off one of the most poignant discoveries of my life — one which would leave me totally and permanently changed!

*For additional truth concerning God's Will To Heal . . .see Part II.

CHAPTER SIX.....

GOD'S KEY
FOR MY HEALING!

I truly praise God for letting me get to that Kathryn Kuhlman service, because I entered that service a "saved", "born-again" believer knowing that I was going to meet Jesus when I died. I knew Jesus *as Saviour:* I had the faith in Him to die, but I didn't know Him *as Healer* and consequently I had no faith at all to be healed!

Although I hadn't yet seen all this truth concerning Jesus as Healer, I did know that what I had witnessed in that service didn't "jibe" with my theology. Since I couldn't bend the facts that I had seen, I knew that it was my theology that was going to have to be bent, or straightened out!

I came out of that service convinced of two things: first I wanted to get to a doctor and get an X-Ray to see if perhaps I had been one of the lucky ones healed without even knowing it. I had no sensation of pain at that time with the tumor in my left lung, and wouldn't have known if it was gone. I wanted to have an X-Ray done because the odds seemed better than they had ever been, that I might have been healed. The second thing that I wanted to do was to get into the Scriptures to find out what God's word had to say regarding my healing. Obviously there was something that I had been missing.

I did have the X-Ray and then I got a copy of the *Good News* and I studied the healings all through the New Testament, underlining them with a blue pencil. Like many another person, I too, wound up with a blue Bible!

* * * * * * *

I found, and you will find the same thing, that Jesus healed every person who came to Him seeking healing! He healed them all, without exception, and He healed somewhat indiscriminantly, it would seem, by our standards. *Everyone that came to Him was healed.* Although most of them were healed right on the spot, instantly, some were first required to take a "step of faith" like the woman with the flow of blood. All she did was to touch the hem of His garment and she was instantly healed. I was fascinated by the fact that Jesus didn't have to think about healing her, nor pray about it, nor even have a consultation with the Father about it. The healing just naturally flowed from Him as naturally as warmth and light radiate from the Sun. He did however, require her to take a step of faith in identifying the one who had healed her, and to confess publicly, the fact of her healing!

Consider the fact that Jesus never said to anyone seeking healing, "It isn't the will of God to heal you;" nor, "God isn't through teaching you your lesson;" nor, "I'm sorry, but you don't deserve to be healed." He healed them *all!* Interestingly enough, He is never recorded as praying "Father, is it okay to heal this one?" or, "Should this person be healed?" or, "Have you taught this person everything you wanted them to learn through this sickness?" . . . or any of the other questions we would logically expect Him to have asked, *if it were not the will of God to heal all of His children!*

As I studied the Scriptures, some of them seemed to jump right off the page at me. One of the ministries of the Holy Spirit mentioned in John is that of teacher: He is the One who is to bring to our rememberance the things that Jesus has said; to lead us and guide us into all truth.

One Scripture in particular that really struck me was the account in the thirteenth chapter of Luke of the woman who had been bowed over for eighteen years with some type of disfiguring disease, and who had come to the Synagogue to be healed on the Sabbath day. The rulers of the Synagogue chastised her for coming on the Sabbath. They told her that she had six days in which to come to the Synagogue to be healed, but don't bother us on the Sabbath!

Jesus then rebuked them for criticizing her and said, "Ought not this woman being a daughter of Abraham, whom *Satan* hath bound, lo, these eighteen years, be loosed from this bond?" And he proceeded to heal her right on the spot!

The most *interesting* and *significant* thing in that Scripture for me, was the fact that *Jesus Christ, Himself, identified the specific cause of that particular woman's problem, as Satan!*

When I read that passage, I didn't believe in Satan. In fact, I didn't even know of anyone, in our sophisticated day and age, who did believe in Satan! Satan, I thought, was just a concept that Jesus had come up with in an attempt to communicate with the uneducated, pagan people of His day, who couldn't grasp a more intellectual approach. However, I came to realize that *Jesus did believe* in Satan and I knew I could do no less!

Besides, Jesus never attributed sickness to God, the Father. It was beginning to dawn upon me that *maybe, just maybe, it wasn't God who had wanted me to die of cancer!*

Another Scripture shortly thereafter, seemed to jump

off the page at me also; it was the one where the rulers of the synagogue criticized Jesus for casting out devils, or demons. They accused Him of doing this because He was "In league with Beelzebub," or Satan.

Jesus gave the famous and oft quoted reply, in effect, "You fools, if I was in league with Satan, I wouldn't be casting out Satan." "If a house be divided against itself, that house cannot stand!" (Mt. 12+Mk 3:24ff) I sensed in my heart, that God had more truth to show me in this passage, so I prayed about it and sought Him for understanding, and it came! "*A house divided against itself cannot stand.*" If we turn that around; if illness *were* from God, then the Son of God would not have devoted 80 to 90% of His earthly ministry *to the healing of the physical body,* as He did. He would not have gone against the will of His Father!

Jesus said, "I came . . . not to do mine own will, but the *will of him* that sent me." (Jn. 6:38) "Lo, I come to do *thy will,* O Lord!" (Heb. 10:9) "My meat is to do *the will of him* that sent me." (Jn. 4:34) He also speaks of being "One with the Father," and said also that He "only did those works that He had *seen the Father do.*" "My Father *works hitherto,* and I work." (Jn. 5:17) He knew the will of the Father was *for healing!* God's will for healing is clearly manifested to us in the earthly ministry of Jesus.

In fact the whole Old Testament foreshadows the coming of Jesus Christ *as Healer!* One of the five major compound names of God in the Old Testament is Jehovah-Rapha, which means in Hebrew, "I AM YOUR GOD THAT HEALETH ALL YOUR DISEASES" or "I AM YOUR HEALER!" (Ex. 15:26)

One final example may help us see a great truth. We are prone to play religious games. We repeat, and come to believe, certain pious-sounding things that we've been taught or heard other people say. For example, "My sickness is a blessing in disguise"; or "This sickness is really a blessing from God."

46

Ridiculous! We may think and even say that we believe it, but we really don't! I think I can prove that we don't believe it. What is the first thing that we do when we get sick? We run right out to some doctor and try to get him to take away *the blessing* that God sent us, right? If we *really believed* in our hearts that God had sent the sickness as a blessing, or something *that He wanted us to have,* we would be thanking Him for the sickness and asking Him to send us more. Thus, we already have His truth written in our hearts, that *it is His will for us to be well!*

"Beloved, I wish above all things, that thou mayest prosper and be in health even as thy soul prospereth." (3 Jn. 2)

God Himself identifies Himself as healer! In Exodus 15:26, when He made a covenant with His people for their healing, He said, "If you will diligently hearken to the voice of the Lord your God, and will do what is right in His sight, and will listen to and obey His commandments and keep all His statutes, I will put (or allow to come upon you) none of the diseases which I brought upon the Egyptians; for I am the Lord who heals you." (Ex. 15:26 Amplified Bible) David knew that God was a healer just as He was a Saviour. He states it beautifully in Psalm 103:1-3:

"Bless the Lord, O my soul: and all that is within me, bless His Holy Name.
Bless the Lord, O my soul, and forget not all His benefits:
Who forgiveth all thine iniquities: who healeth all thy diseases."

He doesn't say, "Who healeth *most of,* or *some of* thy diseases, or all thy diseases *except* cancer, or blindness, or diabetes," . . . but says *"ALL* thy diseases!"

The very last Messianic prophecy in the Old Testament comes just a few verses before Malachi ends; "Shall the Sun of Righteousness arise with healing in his wings." (Mal. 4:2)

47

Praise be to God, that's just how Jesus came or I wouldn't be relating this story. The word of God, I found to be so full of the promises for healing that even a stubborn skeptic such as I was, had to begin to yield. God, it seems, had one more puzzle piece of truth for me.

The final element in helping me get over the 'God gave me this cancer' hangup was a story, related originally I believe by Whitehead in his little book, *Will of God*. One day when I was only about half conscious in my hospital room, Sue came in and began relating to me a story about a missionary in India who had gone to visit a man who had just lost his young son to cholera. As they walked on the veranda of the grieving parent's home, he told the missionary, "I can accept it, Padre, for I know *it is the will of God.*"

The missionary said he knew in his heart that he had to say something to convey to the bereaved father that he had misinterpreted God's will. He didn't know how to express it, but then an inspiration came, as he noticed the man's infant daughter sleeping in a mosquito-netting covered cradle on the veranda. He said, "My friend, what would you do if you were to see a man coming up the pathway to your home, carrying in his hand a cottonwad full of cholera germs, and he were to attempt to clamp it over the mouth of your little daughter?"

The father instantly replied, "Why I'd stop him, any way that I could. If I had to, I'd kill him. I wouldn't let him near her. If he did, I'd have him committed to the home for the criminally insane, or put in prison as a murderer!"

The missionary then said softly, "Ah yes, my friend, but then how dare you attribute to God those same attributes that if you found in a man, you'd have him committed as criminally insane or put in prison as a murder?"

The illustration apparently got through to the father, and it also made a deep impression upon me. I realized that God is neither insane, nor a murderer!! But there is one whom Jesus identifies as a liar, a thief and a murderer from the beginning . . . but that *one* is Satan, not God! (John 8:44)

* * * * * * *

The specialist called with the results of the X-Rays taken after the Kuhlman service, stating that they showed the tumor was still there. This news came as a blow to us, because by this time, Sue and I were both believing the promises we'd discovered in the Word of God, and had come to believe that it *was indeed God's will to heal!* Since we both believed, we prayed and asked God *for a miracle.* We prayed for Him to heal me and to do it in such a way that it would be a sign to all the doctors who had been 'hanging crepe' from the beginning, and a sign to many of our friends who had been inclined to accept my condition as being 'God's will.' We wanted God to provide a sign that He was still in the healing business today, just as He had been two thousand years ago!

When you ask God for a miracle, you'd better be prepared! You will probably get it, but it probably won't be in the form you had expected: ours wasn't. I think we had probably expected that there would just be a little "poof", and the tumor would disappear out of my lung. It didn't happen that way!

CHAPTER SEVEN.....

DARKNESS
BEFORE THE DAWN!

In January of 1971, we got our miracle, or the beginning of it: and it *wasn't* in the form we'd expected! The second week of January I became terribly sick. For a week I couldn't keep food down; we thought I had the flu. The following week I was even sicker, and wasn't even able to keep water down. By the end of that week, the specialist called and told me, "Bill, we have to get you back into Barnes Hospital so that we can get some fluids into you, to keep you from dehydrating."

They put me back into Barnes on Friday, the 22nd of January. The date sticks in my mind because that day was to have been the first time Sue and I were going to attend a Full Gospel Business Men's meeting in downtown St. Louis.

We didn't really know very much about the Full Gospel Business Men's Fellowship: On the negative side we had heard that they too, "spoke in tongues"; and on the positive side, we knew that they believed in healing and that they had sponsored a Kathryn Kuhlman meeting in St. Louis the preceeding August; so they couldn't be all bad. We wanted to attend their meeting to see just what they might have to offer.

However, I obviously couldn't go because they readmitted me to the hospital at five o'clock that afternoon. Sue was pretty upset, seeing me go back into Barnes, looking worse than I had when I'd come out after my previous 45-day stay. She was so distraught she said, only half-jokingly "I can either go home and slash my wrists, or go on to the FGMBFI meeting."

As soon as she left my room, they immediately began performing tests upon me. This time I knew there was something really seriously wrong. If you have ever been a patient in a hospital, you have, no doubt, had the experience of having high school kids and others pushing your hospital cart from one part of the hospital to another. All the while they are making small talk, chatting with one another, smoking etc. However this time, something was really wrong, because the *doctors, themselves,* were pushing my cart and *they were running full speed* down the halls of the hospital! Now that really isn't the sort of thing that inspires confidence in the state of one's health!

They did tests on me throughout the night, with the technicians all grumbling about having to work at 12:00 and 1:00 A.M.

The following morning, Sue came into my room and said she had gone to the FGBMI meeting and had enjoyed it. She told of hearing the testimony of a Catholic psychology professor who had received the Baptism in the Holy Spirit and how it had changed and blessed his life. She also mentioned that afterwards a prayer room was made available to which she went requesting prayer for my healing. I told her "Praise God!" I knew I needed all the prayer I could get.

"But then," she continued, "the Catholic psychology professor laid his hands upon my head, and told me to stop speaking in English. I did," she marveled, "and I began to speak in tongues."

I wasn't sure at that point which one of us was delirious, but I was pretty sure that it wasn't me! I often told Sue the reason that she received the Baptism in the Holy Spirit three months before I did, was due to the fact that she didn't know the Bible as well as I did, and that her theology wasn't as good as mine!

Sue hadn't stopped to try to analyse her "tongues". She was too desperate. She pragmatically used the language which she had received and was blessed thereby. She had prayed again in her new language when she went to bed that night, and found to her surprise that she was *able to go to sleep without sleeping medication for the first time in four months,* since she had been told that I was going to die of cancer!

The testing continued through Saturday evening. Early Sunday morning the specialist came in to see me and said, "Bill, we have the results back on all these tests we've been doing on you. And the results don't look good! You have six things wrong with you: Any one of them could and *probably should kill you!*

CHAPTER EIGHT.....

SIX BLOWS FROM SATAN!

The doctor's face indicated the seriousness of his visit, as he repeated the details, "You have six things wrong with you: any *one* of the six could and *probably should kill you.*" He paused and then continued, "Your kidneys have stopped completely; your body has completely quit producing new blood cells; you have a red blood cell count of 10,000 (normal is 250,000 — it takes 40,000 to sustain life — you have a count of 10,000); you are hemorrhaging internally — so you are losing what little blood you have left; you have an intestinal obstruction that shows up on the X-rays that we will have to cut out of you before we can give you any food or water — if we can keep you that long? — and the other thing, is that you are jaundicing, and the tests indicate that you have either a total liver malfunction or a total malignancy of the liver! Now those are the six things that you have wrong with you. I can't promise you anything, but *I think we can buy you 48 hours,* if we can get you on a kidney machine!"

He then left me with my thoughts and went to call Sue to bring her up to date. She had been praying at home in the new language which she'd received. The Lord was dealing very beautifully with her and was building her up for what was to follow. As she prayed and praised God in her unknown language, God revealed some insight to her.

That Sunday morning as she went down to breakfast, she met her mother who was staying with her to help with the boys, and she said, "Wouldn't it be terrible if Bill would have to be on a kidney machine for the rest of his life?"

Her mother replied, "What is the matter with you? Are you crazy? There isn't anything wrong with Bill's kidneys!" And there really wasn't so far as we knew, they were working fine when I entered the hospital.

Almost immediately the phone rang. The specialist was calling to tell Sue that I was going to be on the kidney machine. The fact that Sue knew in advance that I was going to be on the kidney machine, so shook him up, that every day after that when he would come in to check on me, he would ask her, "And what do your "vibrations" tell you today?"

I didn't know until years later, how great an additional miracle God had performed for me. Barnes Hospital at that time had only one "emergency" dialysis or kidney machine. Its three other machines were for chronic, or regular patients, who are tightly scheduled to utilize the machines. Since no one else needed it at that precise time, it was available for me. *God's timing was perfect!*

When Sue hung up the phone after talking with the doctor she was able to sit down and eat breakfast with the boys, because of the peace which God had also given her when He had warned her that I was to be on the kidney machine. After breakfast Sue sat in the rocker that we have in our family room and looked out the glass door on the back of our house. As she did, she had a revelation from God in her mind's eye. She saw a huge door, open just slightly, with something very ominous behind it. Then she saw a huge hand reach down and close that door. She interpreted the vision, for herself, to be the *hand of God closing the door on death!*

The fantastic mercy and love of God manifested toward Sue was beautiful and it was so kind of Him to give her peace as He did. It was truly needed because things became extremely bleak in the days that followed. They had me on the kidney machine for 4 days, and gave me 31 blood transfusions. Then the specialist came in to see me and reported, "Bill, we have done everything for you *medically* that we know how to do. There isn't anything else that we can do, short of 'chopping into you and putting pumps in you to keep you going' and that sort of thing. I don't want to do that, and besides, we've been able to get your blood count up to about 38,000 with all the transfusions and I think we can hold you for a while. So I think that we'll just wait."

Now that sounded like an ideal framework within which the Lord could move and get all the glory for what would happen. When medical science had done everything it knew how to do, and had admitted that it didn't have anything else to do in my case; it was going to be clear that if I got healed, it was the Lord's doing and not man's. (Psalm 109:27)

At first I thought that the Lord had waited to that point for the benefit of the doctors, to give them a sign. But the sign wasn't for the doctors, because apparently only one out of the five or more involved, really accepted what happened as a miracle. The rest attempted to pass it off as a mysterious working of medication or another "mysterious remission", an unexplained case, or who knows what.

I now believe that the Lord delayed my healing until medical science had exhausted its capabilities, so that *I* would know beyond any shadow of a doubt whom it was that had healed me, and that *you* might know also! Some of those doctors involved directly or indirectly with my

57

case may still be skeptical, some may still be atheists or agnostics. They were not brought by the situation to a saving confrontation with the Living Christ nor forced to acknowledge Him as Healer, as I had hoped that they might.

To give an indication of how really bleak my situation was: one of the young doctors whom I had met while in the hospital, who had been involved in some of my treatment, came to see Sue one evening during the week I was on the kidney machine. As he was talking with her he broke down and he began to cry, "Sue, I've come to love that guy. Don't let him suffer anymore than he already has." He implied that she should take me off the machine and let me just go.

As you can imagine that would normally have devastated her, yet God was working in and upon her, and she was able to turn to him and say, "Yes but, God is going to heal him!"

Our battle wasn't constantly victorious, however. One night after spending the entire day upon the kidney machine, I was wheeled back up to my room. I really felt drained. The only way I could later describe the sensation of being on the kidney machine, was to say that I felt as if I had been swimming upstream in a fast river all day. I felt as if every ounce of strength that I possessed had been drained right out of me. I could barely turn my head from side to side. Sue met my cart in the hallway and when I looked at her face I knew she was hurting for me. She had held up pretty well throughout our ordeal, rarely crying in my presence. The young doctor had just left her and she was down. She said defeatedly, "I've done all I can. I give up, I'm just going to ask the Lord to take you. You've suffered too much already."

I was hurting for her and I began telling her, "Don't do that! Don't ask the Lord to take me! I'm not really hurting that much, and besides if I do die, tell them that I love Jesus. God is so good, don't let anyone blame God for what Satan is putting me through. If I die tell them that I love God."

I don't really know who the "they" were that I spoke of, but I didn't want anyone speaking ill of my Lord whom I loved. I was so filled with love for Him at that moment that nothing else really mattered to me. It was a very emotional scene and I'm sure the nurses who were respectfully averting their eyes as they passed, must have thought we were crying over my condition, and yet it wasn't pity . . . it was more joy in Him than anything else.

A day or so later, God responded and sovereignly began moving to heal me; that afternoon he started my kidneys, later that same night he apparently started my body to producing blood cells again. He also stopped the hemorrhaging because the following morning my blood count had jumped from under 40,000 where they had been able to get it with all the transfusions, to well over 90,000, almost 95,000, which amazed the doctors. For the blood count to increase like it did involved about a three-fold miracle. The body had to start producing new blood cells, the kidneys had to function, and the hemorrhaging had to stop before it could increase.

After three days of observing my blood counts, the team of specialists sent word, "We think you now have enough blood that your body can withstand an operation, so we'll whack this obstruction out of your intestines. Then we can give you the food and water you've been clamoring for." I hadn't been able to have water since the obstruction was detected.

Sue plaintively begged of the surgeon who was to remove the obstruction, "Isn't there any possible way you can spare that poor guy another operation? Isn't there some way that the obstruction could just dissolve itself?"

He said brusquely, "There is no way! Apparently when we did the big operation, we damaged the walls of the intestine and this knot or adhesion has grown. We will have to cut it out in order for anything to pass through. It won't go away by itself!"

They wheeled me on my "Rolling Stretcher" down to the X-Ray department, pumped me full of "chalk," wheeled me in and took their pictures. I was then wheeled out into the hall again to await the developing of the X-Rays. The specialist who was to do the operation came up to my stretcher and began poking upon me, apparently to determine where he was going to cut. About ten minutes later the technicians came out with the X-Rays and said, "These X-Rays are no good! We'll have to take them over again."

Whereupon, the specialist said a few unkind things about the X-Ray department, as they wheeled me back in for more pictures. They wheeled me out again a few minutes later. The specialist was still waiting and began once again to poke and probe. After about another ten or fifteen minutes the technicians returned to report, "These X-Rays are no good either! They look just like the last ones; that thing isn't there anymore!"

With that the specialist threw his hands in the air and said, "In that case, you don't need *me!*" and he walked down the hall of the hospital shaking his head.

They observed me for a few more weeks in the hospital. The liver tests showed completely normal and each of the six things that were "supposed to kill me" was taken care of by the Lord in His own time, when the doctors had given up.

I was released from the hospital on February 26th, 1971, with the tumor still in my left lung. By that time they had thrown everything that they had at it. They had blasted my chest with a maximum dosage of 25 treatments of cobalt, and beta-tron (which is stronger than cobalt) and even used chemo-therapy or drug therapy on me. All apparently to no avail. As one of the doctors put it, "Nothing we have has ever proven effective against the type of cancer which you have, but we're trying all these drugs and radiation in the hope that somehow in combination they might help."

When they released me on the 26th, I went home and became further convinced of the possibility that this Satan character might really exist. My resistance was apparently low, and I came down with the flu three times. Then my two boys managed to get themselves exposed to chicken-pox which they didn't catch, but I caught what adults get, who've already had chicken pox. I got the shingles and developed the worst case of it that my doctor said he had ever seen. It would take two handkerchiefs to cover the scars down the right side of my body around the area of my hip. For about a month, I was flat on my back barely able to move because it felt like my right hip was out of its socket. The following month and a half, half-dollar sized blisters formed and I felt as if people were putting out cigars on my right side!

All of my physical problems and weakness didn't bode too well for my being able to make the third jaunt in our search for the "Holy Grail" of healing, which was to be a trip to the Tennessee-Georgia C.F.O.* We wanted to attend this particular week-long meeting for several reasons. We knew that these people believed in healing, and had reported miracles having occurred at their camps, and we heard that Derek Prince was to be one of their speakers.

Another thing that Sue had "tormented" me with while I was trying to "quietly die of cancer" was Derek Prince cassette tapes. Derek is a tremendously intelligent man, and an outstanding scholar. He was educated at Eton College and King's College Cambridge where he was elected to a Fellowship, and where he served as, in effect, Professor of

Philosophy and Logic. He preaches in seven languages, has been a missionary on five continents; has taught Hebrew to the Hebrews and Greek to the Greeks. In a recent newspaper article, it was stated that he is felt to be one of the most brilliant men to have graduated from Cambridge in over three hundred years.

However, when you hear his tapes as I did, first thing in the morning, while you're having breakfast; hear him while you're having lunch; and the last thing that you hear before you fall asleep at night; that's too much. I have since told him so, over which we both had a good laugh.

I was impressed with the obvious brilliance of this man, and with the clarity of his teaching upon the tapes that Sue played incessantly, and was therefore receptive when Sue suggested that we might go to hear him. I was eager to hear him in person, and to see what help he might be able to add in the way of teaching or ministry in my search for healing.

*Camps Farthest Out is an inter-denominational organization which believes in the power of prayer, and has found that miracles happen when small groups pray and fellowship together in New Testament fashion in camp meetings.

CHAPTER NINE.....

ANOTHER DOOR OPENS!

God had already shown us that we were to attend this meeting, however the physical circumstances didn't look too promising for our being able to make the trip to Georgia. I hadn't been out of the house since I'd returned home from the hospital and was barely able to totter from the sofa in the family room to the kitchen for meals. Five days before the day we were scheduled to leave, it suddenly struck me that if the Lord were to somehow work a "miracle" and get me out of the house so that I could make the trip, I would have to get a hair-cut since I hadn't had one in over 5 months. I asked Sue to drive me to a barber shop which she did. The exertion of sitting in the barber's chair, however, so exhausted me that I had to go home and lie flat on my back for the rest of the day.

That evening I received a call from a man, later to become a dear and close friend, Bill Moorman. Bill was a Presbyterian minister and a member of the St. Louis Full Gospel Business Men's chapter. Bill told me, "Bill, there is an ex-Lutheran minister, Rodney Lensch, who will be speaking at your church tomorrow evening. He believes in healing. Why don't you go and hear him, and have him pray for your healing and strength to make the trip to Georgia?"

I told him that I would, if I could possibly make it. I then told Sue about the conversation and asked her if she'd like to go. She said, "I've heard Rod give his testimony several times already, why don't you get your folks to take you?"

When I called my folks, they as always, responded in a loving way and offered to pick me up and both agreed to attend the meeting with me.

* * * * * * *

One of the things that had helped me overcome my prejudices against tongues . . . was the reading of a book. A book that I happened to finish the day that I received the call from Bill Moorman, inviting me to hear Rod Lensch's testimony. *The timing of God is perfect!* The book was entitled *They Speak With Other Tongues* written by John Sherrill, then senior editor of Guideposts Magazine. Sherrill had apparently been given a contract to write a book disproving the phenomenon of people speaking in tongues. The first eighty percent of the book deals with his unsuccessful attempts to disprove tongues with linguistic experts, tape recordings and the like. The last twenty percent relates his own experiences after he had himself received the Baptism in the Holy Spirit.

There is a beautiful anointing of the Lord upon the material included in this book. At several points as I was reading the book, I found tears to be welling up in my eyes, as the Lord drove His Truth home to my heart! Often since, as I have traveled around the country, I have heard people testify, "Just before I received, I was reading a book. I'd read a little bit, and then I'd cry a little, and then I'd read some more; and cry some more." Invariably, the book referred to, turned out to be Sherrill's *They Speak With Other Tongues*.

As I read the book, and reread the passages of Scripture that related to the Baptism, I became convinced that this was something that God had validly done in the past. Since He is the same yesterday, today and forever, He wouldn't have changed now, I reasoned. Therefore I decided that tongues must then be valid for today as well. Even though I *doubted that it was for me,* I knew it was valid, and something that God was still doing.

In light of this reasoning, I came to the point that I was at least willing to receive the Baptism *with tongues!* If God chose to bless me with His Baptism and with the tongues that seemed to be such a part of it, I was finally *willing to receive it!* I was finally *open* to speaking in tongues. I wasn't eager to, but willing to. My rationale was somewhat close to, "If God wants me to speak in tongues, and that is to be the 'initiatory rite' through which I must somehow pass, before I could really go on with Him, into whatever more of a "walk" He had for Me, *I was willing!* I wanted to go on with Him even more than I wanted my own self-respect, or pride in not doing anything so apparently irrational as speaking in tongues.

I was unable to see *God's perfect timing* in this situation also, until I looked back in retrospect . . . but perfect timing it was! Within twenty-four hours, after completing the book and becoming open, I was invited to the meeting at which I was to receive the Baptism in the Holy Spirit!

* * * * * * *

The next evening, promptly but rather shakily I walked into the little carpeted lounge off the chapel in our church where Rod Lensch was to speak, and was greeted by several friends. Although their greetings were hearty, you can always tell when you really look bad . . . no one will look you in the eye, if they can help it! All those dear saints at church would avert their eyes, so as to prevent my seeing in their expressions, how really bad they felt that I looked! To make matters worse, as soon as they felt I wasn't looking, they began edging away from me . . . as if they were afraid that I was going to die on the spot and might hit them as I fell.

That Wednesday evening, Rod gave his testimony of how he had received the Baptism in the Holy Spirit and how it had changed his life and ministry. It was moving and challenging to those present. When he completed his presentation, I introduced myself to him and explained that I had come for prayer. He said, "Oh, yes, you're Sue's husband." (a designation that took months to live down).

Almost before I was aware of what was happening, he had whisked me into a small adjoining anteroom. He then pulled a vial of oil out of his pocket and anointed my head, laid his hands upon me and began to pray for my healing and strength to make the trip to Georgia. Then when he had completed his prayer, he turned to me and asked, "Bill, have you received the Baptism in the Holy Spirit?"

I attempted to explain to him about all the people out in North Carolina who had prayed for me and over me apparently to no avail. "But," he interrupted, "let's not worry about that: let's just ask the Lord right now to Baptize you with the Holy Spirit."

So I bowed my head. He asked; I asked; and apparently the Lord did Baptize me, because I then uttered two gutteral syllables that I couldn't understand. Now I must confess in all honesty, that I didn't really care for either syllable. They both sounded to me like something an African tribesman might utter while poking his fire, and I couldn't see how that could possibly be of any benefit to the Lord! However on the off chance that this might have been what the Lord was speaking of, when he said, "Believers shall speak with new tongues". I determined to use it, in faith, until He gave me something better.

Rod said, "Praise God, that's it! You have received the Baptism in the Holy Spirit!"

When I got home I told Sue who immediately exclaimed, "Praise God, that's it! You have received the Baptism in the Holy Spirit!"

He was ecstatic, she was ecstatic, but I was extremely in doubt that anything had taken place. I had had *absolutely no experiential confirmation* that what I'd received had been valid, or from God, even though I knew that I was not prone to be emotional, nor to get "psyched up".

Saturday morning I got in the car and drove Sue and I to Georgia. We are so prone to not give God the credit: I arrived at the C.F.O. camp in Georgia thinking, "Boy did I recover quickly." *Forgive me, Lord!*

After eating dinner in the dining hall, I returned to the cabin in the state park where we were staying. Sue decided to go on to hear the evening speaker in the main auditorium. I was pretty tired and still weak (in fact so weak that while we were at the camp, they would provide a chair for me to rest in while I was in line waiting to get into the dining hall.) I recall sitting on the bed that night just before I fell asleep, worrying about Kevin and Steven back home.

If I were to list all the things that Satan did in an attempt to prevent our making the trip to Georgia, it wouldn't be believeable. I'll mention just two: one of the boys' pets died the day before we were to leave; the night before we left, Kevin our oldest boy came down 'very mysteriously' with a fever of 104°. Which incidently we later learned, left him, just as 'mysteriously,' the very moment we arrived at the camp.

Satan has fought us every time God was about to reveal more of Himself to us. Whenever God was going to bless us, teach us, or use us . . . Satan fought. In the early days, he would almost invariably attack me physically. Yet he isn't too smart, apparently, because he always winds up *overplaying* his hand.

I sat on the bed, thinking to myself, "Here I am separated, somewhat unnecessarily, for a week from the two boys whom I love more than anything else in the world: with a tumor in my left lung: still under sentence of death." Anticipating a much longer and more permanent separation, I dropped off to sleep.

The next thing I knew, the door to the cabin where we were staying burst open, slamming into the wall. Sue rushed into the room, breathlessly shouting, "Get up quick! Get up quick, we've got to go!"

Somewhat foggily, I said, "What's wrong? What's happened to the boys?"

She said, "There's nothing wrong with the boys. Now come on! Come on! Pull your pants on over your pajamas, and come on. We've got to go!"

"We've got to go?" I queried, "We've got to go *where*?"

"Hurry up and pull your pants up, we've got to go. *You're going to be healed!*"

CHAPTER TEN.....

MIRACLES
AND MORE MIRACLES!

"I'm going to be *healed?*" I asked incredulously, "I'm going to be healed *of what?*"

I had so many things wrong with me that I was afraid someone was going to ask me what I wanted to be healed of, and I'd give him the wrong answer.

Sue interrupted my thoughts with, "Come on, you're going to have your back healed!"

"My *back?*" I responded in utter disbelief. That's like praying for a hangnail, when you're dying of cancer! I had forgotten that about ten years before I'd been rear-ended in an auto accident and that my back had since bothered me off and on if I were to stand for very long.

So we hopped in the car and drove over to the canteen in the state park. As we entered the large bright room, my eyes took in the scene. People were sitting around drinking coffee, eating hot dogs and such, while over in one end of the room a large group of people were in a circular formation, every once in a while raising their arms into the air and exclaiming, "Praise God!" and "Praise the Lord!"

Sue and I moved over to where the action was taking place and I raised myself up on my toes and looked over the heads of the crowd, out into the center of the circle. There I saw, to my surprise, the fabulous scholar, whom I mentioned before, Derek Prince squatting upon the floor in what he himself describes as a 'rather unscholarly' position *holding people's feet!*

The almost unbelievable thing to me was that as he was holding people's feet, people with unequal length limbs would have their legs grow out so that their legs were equal. The first man we observed, sitting in the chair, had a three inch wooden heel built up on the heel of his shoe. As Derek held his feet, his legs began "growing out" until they were perfectly even. Derek then told him to, "Go chop the wooden heel off your shoe, before you throw your back out."

We watched essentially the same thing happen to about fifteen or twenty people. Then I became aware of the same uncomfortable sensation that I'd had back at my church, as I noticed people all around the circle nudging one another and going "Pssst-Pssst" and gesturing toward me with their eyes and a nod of their heads.

I then realized that Sue had been talking at dinner and I had already become the camp's "Healee!" The group began motioning and urging me to sit in the chair and let Derek pray for me. I complied, but as I did I thought to myself, "Boy he has 'booked a loser' this time, because my feet are fine!"

To my surprise, my right leg proved to be about an inch and a half shorter than my left. I wasn't aware of it, nor had it ever troubled me to my knowledge, but the difference was clearly visible. (Prov. 26:7-b)

As Derek held my feet in the palms of his hands, I could feel the bones beginning to move in my right hip. There was no pain at all but I could feel *the bones grating across one another in my right hip as they moved.* I knew that there was no way that his having held my feet like a footstool could make the bones in my hip move. There had to be another *power* involved.

70

The next thing I knew the people all around the circle began praising God because my leg had lengthened, and my heels were now right together. As I stood upright out of the chair I found I was able to take a full deep breath for the first time since the big operation which had left me somewhat hunched over.

Then Sue sat in the chair. Her left leg was about a half inch shorter than her right, and it grew right out. Then Derek said, "Say, are you aware that you have a crooked left leg?"

She wasn't but she was wearing a pants suit that evening, and everyone could see that as she faced the wall straight ahead of her, her left knee pointed to the wall on her left. Derek spoke reassuringly, "Don't worry about it. I think the Lord will heal that too."

Sure enough, as we watched, that left knee cap rotated right straight up! Sue exclaimed that it felt to her as if a big hand had grabbed her whole leg and rotated it all the way up to her hip.

I knew one thing for sure; we were going to get our 'money's worth' out of this camp. All this had happened, the very first night!

The following evening, as you might surmise, I managed to get to the evening meeting to hear the evening speaker. After the speaker had spoken, they made an announcement, "We are going to keep the lights on here in the auditorium, and we have brought in some kneeling rails from a nearby church. If any of you would care to come forward and pray for a deeper commitment, a deeper walk with the Lord, or to be used in some type of ministry, please feel free to stay and pray."

Sue and I were seated toward the back of the auditorium, and by the time we got down to the front the crowd had pretty well thinned. We knelt and prayed for a deeper commitment, a closer walk with the Lord, and to be used in some type of team ministry. As we stood to our feet from the kneeling rail, it was as if we both had magnets within our chests drawing us toward the center aisle. We looked and noticed there a man in a wheel chair whom we hadn't seen before. We later learned that his name was Paul, he was 35 years old; he'd been in an iron lung for two years, and three years in the wheel chair. He was virtually paralyzed; hands locked shut, nails dug into his palms, he could wiggle his elbows about one inch, his head was all scrunched down into his chest, he could speak with difficulty. Paul wasn't attending the camp but had been brought over to the state park by a nurse at a nearby home for the chronically ill, because she had heard that miracles were happening at the camp.

Sue and I both felt that we had to go lay hands upon him and pray for him to be healed. However, neither Sue nor I had ever dared to presume to lay hands upon anyone and to think that the Lord might be able to use that to impart a blessing to them. Even though the Word of God says that *believers* "shall lay hands upon the sick, and they shall recover," (Mk 16:17,18) we'd never had the faith to do it.

Beautifully enough, the Lord managed to deal with our doubts, and was able to get us where He wanted us. We laid our hands upon Paul's shoulders and began praying for him to be healed. We weren't alone. There was also a group of the "Jesus kids" present. One of them sticks in my mind, a little girl about 14, who was praying in tongues for Paul.

About a minute after we began praying, the power of God struck Paul with more force than I could have generated. If I had hit him in the face with everything I had, the best day I lived, I could not have caused the physical reaction that took place in his body when the Power of God struck him. He was seated in the wheel chair, hunched slightly forward. When the Power of God struck him ... He was violently thrown back in the wheelchair almost upsetting it; his arms flew up over his head, and he shouted "Praise you, Jesus!" Then he slumped back down into the wheelchair.

About a minute later, the Power of God struck him again; and again he flew back in the wheel chair with his arms up over his head; and this time his hands opened to about 80% of fully open. As he slumped back into his chair, I heard Sue whisper over my left shoulder, "Have them raise the flaps on his wheel chair."

I directed one of the "Jesus kids" to raise the feet flaps on his wheel chair, so that his feet could actually touch the floor. Almost instantly the third jolt of that heavenly power hit him. He flew back again, and this time, you could hear his spine pop all the way up! Just like someone popping their knuckles, only louder: Pop . . . pop . . . pop . . . pop . . . pop . . . pop all the way up his spinal column. He slumped back down in the wheel chair, and then just as the Scripture states, "Then shall the lame man leap as an hart." (Isa. 35:6) Paul leaped out of the wheelchair onto his feet and *stood upright!*

For the first time in five years, he was on his feet! Yet he didn't struggle to his feet as one might expect. He *leaped* just as the Scripture says. He stood there for perhaps a minute and a half, or two minutes and then, I think, much like Peter walking upon the water, he looked down and thought, "this can't be happening to me." He collapsed in a heap.

Some of the stronger youngsters got him back into his chair. The next thing I knew, my wife was around in front of him stroking his right hand. "Can you feel this?"

He said, "Yes, Ma'am!"

She followed with "Did you have feeling in your hands when you came in here tonight?"

He said, "No more feeling than in the arm of this wheelchair" as he struck the wooden arm rest with his fist.

Sue then continued, "The Holy Spirit is working in your

body tonight, and He is not through. He is going to continue to work through your body for another two or three days."

My immediate, unspoken reaction to her statement was, "What on earth are you telling this poor guy?"

Nevertheless, I should have realized that she would not have had the audacity to have said it, had she not indeed been inspired to say it. (Sure enough two nights later, they had what they called a "healing service" in the camp. They instructed anyone desiring healing to come up onto the stage where they had a minister stationed, who would say a brief prayer as he laid a hand upon the person. For those who weren't instantly healed they also had forty or fifty ministers and priests from various denominations lined up in front of the stage on floor level, who would pray with each individual about his specific need.

Paul got just to the center of the stage in his wheelchair (I was acutely aware of his position in the line, as I was ahead of him, and the person pushing his wheelchair kept cutting me in the ankles with his wheel flaps.) When the minister touched him, Paul again leaped to his feet, walking and laughing. He circled the stage twice, and then took a front aisle seat. From that point on, whenever anyone attempted to go up the center aisle, Paul would grab them by the sleeve, and yell, "Hey look, brother," and would proceed to wave his arms and legs, in demonstration of the miracle which God had performed upon his physical body!

We saw a number of fantastic things happen in that camp. One other high point began the same night that Paul first jumped out of his wheelchair. When Paul stood to his feet, I noticed as I looked past him, a young woman sitting on the kneeling rail with tears streaming down her cheeks. The tears didn't really mark her as unique, for there were tears streaming down the cheeks of everyone present, that night, skeptics included. I was, however, touched by the woman's involvement in the scene, even though just an onlooker. I also noticed that she had to be helped up from the kneeling rail. I later learned that she had had her left knee cap surgically removed, and wore long dresses to cover the scars around her knee.

The next morning on the way to breakfast, a beautiful brother in the Lord, a Baptist minister, Floy Cox grabbed my arm and said, "Praise God, Bill! I've just seen the first mini-skirt I've ever seen to the glory of God!"

I asked him what he was talking about, but he would only say, "Go to the dining hall and see for yourself."

When I arrived at the dining hall I discovered a group of people gathered around this young woman, examining her knee. *The Lord had given her a new knee cap over night!*

Apparently her faith had been built by seeing what the Lord had done for Paul, and she and the women in her cabin had prayed for one another in a general sort of way later that night. God had *overnight,* given her "the desire of her heart" (Psalm 37:4) or perhaps done something beyond her ability to "ask or think." (Eph. 3:20) I was there as a doctor from the Bethesda Naval Academy poked and probed and palpitated the kneecap in utter amazement. He turned with tears dripping down his face and asked, "How do you get this power?"

These fantastic displays of God's miraculous power having been manifested, we couldn't have expected more to happen . . . but it did!

CHAPTER ELEVEN.....

"DŌRON"

Sue was concerned about the fact that I was not entirely satisfied with the new language that I had received. Thus while we were attending the camp, she suggested that it might be advantageous for me to sit down and counsel privately with one of the speakers at the camp. She asked if I would be willing if she could set it up. I finally agreed, but was still so weak that I told her she would have to make all the arrangements.

The next day she returned to our room elated with news; "I've asked Charles Simpson if he'd be willing, and he has said that he will meet you tonight right after dinner."

After dinner I met with Charles Simpson, to whom I had already taken a liking. I was impressed with his soft spoken, easy-going honest manner, and he struck me as one of those people who just seem to exude the joy and love of the Lord. We walked a little way from the dining hall, and he suggested that we sit on a secluded concrete park bench located under overhanging pine trees. He shared with me briefly about the Baptism of the Holy Spirit and how natural it was, and how we needed only to drink in of His Spirit to receive. He then suggested that I drink deeply of the Spirit as we prayed, and then urged me to use my language, or to 'pray in tongues.' I prayed aloud with him using my "language." Even though it had in the week of usage gotten only slightly smoother sounding. I still didn't feel any of the things I'd heard people were supposed to feel. However, he seemed pleased and encouraged me to keep on using what I had. Although I hadn't felt any anointing, I did feel *a real peace,* sitting and praying with this very gracious new brother in-the-Lord.

Toward the end of our week in Georgia, I found the worship and singing in the camp to be tremendously uplifting, joyful, and jubilant. One of the things that I had never before experienced was being in a service where people began to "sing in tongues" (I Cor. 14:15), or to "worship *in the Spirit*". Although I am not in the least bit musical, I found both the singing and the Spirit infectious and really desired to participate.

I had, in fact, hated to sing since grade school where my "poor-singing" career began. By the time I was in college my singing was so bad I had become something of a legend. So bad in fact, my college fraternity offered to pay my way to the picture show in town the night of the campus inter-fraternity sing! I wasn't sensitive about my inability to sing, I just *didn't sing!*

However, as I heard the joyful singing of the people in the camp I found that there was joy in my heart too, and I wanted to sing and praise the Lord in song. The songs were joyful and easy to sing. I did enter into the singing in English and felt it was some of the most meaningful worship in which I had ever participated.

I had nevertheless, merely sat reverently while the others had been worshipping the Lord by singing "in the Spirit". Not really knowing how to, but feeling that I would like to enter into the beautiful worshipping in the Spirit, I asked the Lord for a word that I could sing while the others were singing so beautifully in their "prayer languages". Since I wasn't even convinced that I could speak in tongues, it wasn't a faith-filled prayer, but I did ask and a word came into my mind. It was the word, "*Doron*" or "*Dorean*". I was surprised at how beautifully the word fit in with the tune being played by the man playing the piano in the spirit, and the tune sung by the rest of the people. My "do-ron", "do-ron,", "dor-ean" somehow seemed to fit perfectly into the rising and falling pitches of the music. I was so impressed with the word that I wrote it down in my notes, and showed it to Sue after the service.

I was convinced that it was merely something that I had made up. It didn't feel any more like a real word, or like "tongues" to me than had any other word. However, I was really impressed with the way the Lord had, at least, answered my prayer and let me have a word with which to worship.

* * * * * * *

Nearly two years later, taking first year Greek, I was flabbergasted to find in our vocabulary list, the word "*Doron*" (and upon checking further, the variation "*Dorean*"). I learned that this is the Greek word for *Gift*. In the New Testament, when reference is made to an undeserved, unearnable gift, such as the *gift of salvation,* or *the gift of the Spirit,* the word for gift always used is this word *Doron,* which carries the connotation of a birthday gift. There is nothing that you or I can do to earn a birthday gift! By virtue of the fact that we are alive, and someone loves us, they give us a birthday gift. There is nothing that we can do to earn it, or to become more deserving of it. It is a gift. This perfectly symbolizes grace, and especially God's gracious, gift of the Holy Spirit!

God had given me a word, in tongues! A proveable word. A word that seemed to, so beautifully, symbolize . . . that which He was indeed giving to me and to all who were willing to receive . . . the *gift* of His Holy Spirit.

And *"Ye shall receive the gift of the Holy Ghost"* (Acts 2:38)

* * * * * * *

Shortly after my meeting with Charles Simpson, Sue met someone at camp who had another 'theory' about how *to really receive* the Baptism. This person told her that the way you got freedom in your prayer language, was to get fully relaxed in a *bath tub full of hot water!*

When Sue told me about this as we left camp heading for home, it really didn't seem to make a lot of sense, but I was willing to try anything at that point. The more I thought about the prospect of having a language, and being *sure of it,* the faster I found myself driving. It must have been a ludicrous sight to the heavenly powers looking on; the pale, skinny guy and his wife racing toward Chattanooga, Tennessee to find a bathtub!

As soon as we found a promising looking motel, and I had dragged our luggage inside, I headed for the bathroom, shedding clothes like Clark Kent. I immersed myself, anticipating a spiritual experience, but to my disappointment, I found that I didn't feel one bit more anointed in the hot tub of water, than I had before entering it. I determined not to waste either the hot water, or the time of privacy which He had provided. I decided to boldly make a request of God: "God, you are the author of all languages. You are an infinite Creator. I'm going to ask you right now to give me more language, a new language or more freedom in my 'language'. I am going to go through our alphabet, I'll make an "A" sound, a "B" sound, a "C" sound and so forth, and I'm going to ask you to give me a new word starting with each sound."

80

The words that God provided me, didn't sound any more spiritual to me than any of the others that I had spoken, previously, but I seemed to gain freedom, at least, in letting sounds that I didn't know the meaning of to come out of my mouth. Our minds tend to fight our speaking in tongues, because our minds have spent a lifetime trying to prevent our letting things come out of our mouths that we don't understand, or that might cause us to be ridiculed.

I mention this account of my bathtub experience, to illustrate the extremes to which people seeking the Baptism are apt to go when not properly instructed, or taught. It is essential that we offer clear teaching about the Baptism. We should not be double-minded about the Baptism, or whether tongues are important, or of God, or an essential part thereof. We need to be fully persuaded and to have our hearts fixed.

We cannot receive anything of God we do not know to be the will of God. This is a formula-like statement that the Lord gave me several years ago. To state it negatively may help us see its truth. We can't expect God to do anything we think He *doesn't want to do.* Thus, we need to search the Scripture and establish firmly in our hearts His promise and His will to give a personal private devotional language to His children.

As we set out for home, we knew that we had moved from the stage of seeking God for help for ourselves and into a stage of serving Him. We knew God had called us, and even though I had no proof yet that my lung was free of cancer, Sue and I resolved to share the truths we had been shown concerning the reality of the Holy Spirit with all who would listen. God provided such listeners in dramatic and beautiful ways in the weeks that followed.

CHAPTER TWELVE.....

WE BEGIN SHARING
THE GOOD NEWS!

We returned to St. Louis from Georgia and for the next four weeks it was as if the Lord had set up a social schedule for us. We had only one night in the entire month that followed our return when we weren't either in someone else's home sharing about the miracles we had seen or had people arrive at our own home. We had nothing to do with the setting up or arranging of any of it, it just happened. We would share with them the wonderful experiences we had had with people, the miracles of God's healing power which we had witnessed, and the fantastic displays of His power we had seen.

The Lord then provided a one week period of rest and catching up on sleep for us. The flow of people to our home just dried up and so we rested. On the next Saturday morning, about an hour after breakfast, I went upstairs without saying anything to anyone and "lost" my breakfast. I attempted to conceal the fact from Sue because I knew it would upset her and I thought she would interpret it as a return of the side-effects of the cobalt treatment. I was laying across our bed still feeling rather queasy and I'm sure looking very green, as she came into the bedroom. She took one look at me, and asked if I'd been sick. I nodded. Her reaction was not at all what I'd expected. She said,

"Something wonderful is going to happen." *Satan always overplays his hand.*

Within five minutes of her making that comment, before she could even leave the room, the phone rang. It was a young minister calling to see if we'd be willing to come that evening and share the story of what we'd experienced with a small group in a private home. Sue looked at me, green and sprawled across the bed, and "filled with compassion for me," said, "Sure, we'll be there at 8:00 P.M."

Satan fought that evening until the very moment I was to stand up and speak. I was, in fact, just leaning over to ask the host for the location of the bathroom because I felt I was about to be sick, when he said, "Come on, Bill, tell us about these miracles you and Sue have seen."

So I began to share with them, and as soon as I did, Satan's attack of nausea left. After Sue and I had shared our story with them, I happened to mention that the "leg-lengthening ministry" which we had observed in Georgia had followed us back to St. Louis and that we had seen people healed in exactly the same way.

That apparently prompted a young man present to say, "Hey Bill, I have a medically diagnosed short leg. It has been medically diagnosed as being one and a half inches short. What do you think you can do for me?"

I replied, "Well I know that *I* can't do anything for you, but come sit in a chair and let us pray for you; and we'll see what *Jesus* will do for you."

We seated him in a chair in the middle of the room and all present prayed for him as I held his feet. The inch and a half short leg promptly grew out till both heels matched perfectly. I then had him thank Jesus for healing him. Someone behind me then squealed, "Look at his pants legs . . . his cuffs!"

We did and noticed immediately that one leg of his tailored pants was one and a half inches higher than the other. So it was obvious to every one present that God had indeed lengthened his short leg!

* * * * * *

At that time we really didn't know too much about this "ministry" of holding feet and praying for healing, and as is often the case, we made mistakes. God only gives good and perfect gifts! (James 1:17) However, those who receive the gifts are not perfect, we are all human, fallible, and often stumble along the way. There has only been one perfect person, and that was Jesus. Every person whom God has used before or since has been mortal and prone to the mistakes that flesh is bound to make. This was true in our case, and seeing this truth has helped me to understand how men and women with supernatural ministries have been discovered to have human weaknesses. As I said we made some mistakes. That night since we were new to this "ministry", we agreed when asked, to hold feet and pray for each person in the room. The Lord very graciously lengthened the legs of each person, and healed two people instantly of physical conditions for which they sought prayer. The last person however, was something else. I held one woman's feet and noticed that there was as great a difference in the length of her legs as the first young man had had. I began praying for her and as I did, the leg came out about a quarter of an inch and then it stopped! I kept holding her feet, but nothing was happening. I began to sweat. It seemed like an eternity, but was probably only 5 minutes. I had a quick conversation with the Lord, and said, "Lord, I don't understand this at all. I've never seen this happen. Always before, I've just held the feet and they've come right out. What's wrong here? Besides, Lord, I don't know how to have it not work. What do I do now?"

At that point the Lord had the woman's husband, the

young minister, present, come across the room, to join us by laying his hands upon her and praying also for it to grow out. The leg then seemingly, begrudgingly, came out the remaining inch and a quarter, to be even. A week later in the privacy of his study, the young minister asked me "Would you like to know why my wife's leg didn't move the other night?"

I said, "I sure do! I've never seen God start the healing, and then have it stop like that."

There is a tremendously important lesson here that I want to share with you. Our *minds* have a great deal to do with what happens to us. Bad theology is truly a cruel taskmaster; bad theology can kill. Bad theology told me that Jesus didn't heal today. Therefore I nearly died not realizing that healing was available. Bad theology can kill spiritually. Bad theology says you don't need to accept Jesus as Saviour — thereby denying you eternal life.

He explained, "My wife is a church's organist. And she was afraid that if that leg lengthened an inch and a half, that she would no longer be able to find the keys on the floor key board of the organ. So she made the decision with *her mind* not to let it happen. When I joined in praying she changed her mind and decided to let it happen."

Now I realize that this is offensive theology to us. She made a decision with her mind not to let God move (heal) her legs.

To think that a man can block God is offensive to us theologically. We don't like to think that anyone can limit God. No man can limit God, *Only God can limit God!* However, God has voluntarily limited Himself to operate within the framework of our free wills!!! He doesn't approach the door of your heart with a battering ram, but with a still small voice, and a gentle knock. You and I have to make the decision to invite Him into our hearts. He is too much of a Gentleman to force His way in. We have to make the decision to receive His offer of salvation and eternal life. So too we must, in essence, make the decision with our minds to receive anything else that he offers, healing included. He won't force healing upon anyone who doesn't want to be healed. This truth is indicated in the Scripture, in the seemingly unnecessary question Jesus often asked of afflicted people: "What do you want me to do for you?"

* * * * * *

The fellow who had first had his leg lengthened, wearing the tailored trousers, suddenly put forth a question that really threw me, "Hey, Bill, I want to receive the Baptism in the Holy Spirit. How do you get it? Will you pray for me right now?"

I thought, "Uh-Oh! Neither Sue nor I at that point had ever been called upon to pray for anyone to receive the Baptism in the Holy Spirit and we weren't really sure what to do. However since I felt it wasn't Scriptural to refuse prayer to anyone, I said, "Come and sit in the chair again, and we'll pray for you."

Since I really felt inadequate to the task before us, and since I felt we needed all the prayer power we could muster, I asked the young minister present to join us in laying hands upon him and praying for him. The minister had not yet, himself, received the Baptism, but I felt that his prayers would help. The three of us laid our hands upon the young man and began to pray silently for him. I then led in an audible prayer for him to be Baptized in the Holy Spirit. After we had prayed what I felt was a sufficient length of time, I knelt down beside him and said, "Alright, now just open your mouth and trust the Lord for a whole new language."

He turned and looked at me rather disappointedly and said, "Bill, I don't feel like saying anything!"

I thought, "Oh No! What have we done to the Lord . . . to put Him into an embarrassing situation like this?"

But the Lord is so beautifully faithful . . . He honors our fumbling, bungling, stumbling attempts to minister in His Name: He chose that precise moment to "unload" on the minister. The minister began to shake and to sob. (He shared with me in the privacy of his study a week later, that he knew that he could have spoken in tongues at that moment, but because of some of his parishioners present, he made a *decision with his mind* not to! As an illustration of the love and mercy of God, he subsequently has.) He shared a little later with the group present, that he had felt as if he were totally enveloped in a 'tangible ball of love' and as if he had been lifted right off the floor, and had been floating.

Let me back up just a moment and bring you up to date on my spiritual state at that point. I had been using this gutteral "language" which you will recall I had been given a little over a month before, and had found it to be about as pleasant for me, at first, as having teeth pulled. But I kept on using it in faith; on the off chance that this was what Jesus had promised when He said "believers shall speak with new tongues." I had determined to use this "language" that I had, until He gave me a better one. I had been using the language for a little over a month still with absolutely *zero* experiential confirmation that it was valid, or from God.

Beautifully enough, and perhaps so like the Lord, it was not until I attempted to give away that which I was not entirely sure that I myself, had received, that He in His wisdom, chose to confirm for me, that what I had *was valid,* and *was from Him.*

As Sue and I began praying with the young minister; as he received this touch from the Lord, all of a sudden, I saw a light in the ceiling. My eyes were closed and I was praying in tongues in public for the first time. There were no electric lights in the ceiling of that family room, but suddenly I saw a light in the ceiling and I felt that all the Light and all the Love in the universe was right there, in the ceiling of that family room! I felt as though I had to communicate with that Light. I was standing up on my toes trying to get just as close to that Light as I could. I can't tell you one word that I uttered in tongues that night, except that the same sentence or phrase was repeated at the end. As I was praying I had the distinct feeling as if someone had reached down and grabbed me by the center of my chest; in retrospect, I suspect by the heart, and I felt as though I was bouncing, like on the end of a huge rubber band.

Now you could dismiss my experience as that of someone who'd been psyched up or someone wanting something terribly. I know, however, that I was not psyched up, and for me, this was the experiential confirmation that what I had been doing in faith for a month was valid and was of God!

The joy of experiencing God's calling, and of ministering in His name became reward enough in itself for all that I had suffered in the previous months. The sweetness of His anointing was more than sufficient to erase the reminiscences of past suffering, yet God had one more beautiful surprise in store for me!

CHAPTER THIRTEEN.....

THE
DOCTOR'S LAST WORDS!

Everything was going fine. The blessings of a relationship with the Lord such as I had never before known, crowded most other concerns out of my mind. However, the spectre of the tumor which remained in my left lung continued to show up on the regular X-Rays that were being taken about every month. The doctors had thrown everything they had in their arsenal at it: Cobalt radiation, Beta-Tron, and Chemotherapy, and none had been able to phase it. One of the doctors shared with me that the only reason they were giving me these treatments was that they didn't know what else to do.

While I had been going back to the doctor each month or so for a check up and X-Rays, the tumor had remained the same. Then in June, the doctors suggested a complete physical. They took a complete series of blood tests, X-Rays and the rest. The specialist then announced that he would call me in a day or so with the results.

Two days later the call came. The doctor seemed unusually pleasant and friendly, as he said, "Bill, we've gotten the results back on those tests we did on you. You remember those six things that you had wrong with you back in January of this year?"

I said, "I sure do remember them!"

"Well," he continued, "based upon these tests, no one would know that there had ever been anything wrong with you . . . except for your blood count. You don't have a normal blood count. You have a super-normal blood count. You have a higher blood cell count than most people!"

Praise God! The Lord doesn't do things half-way!

Then the doctor dropped his voice, as people often do when they have some really bad news for you; and he added, " . . . but then we have your *X-Rays!*"

I thought, "Oh my Gosh! Here it comes — those 'clusters of grapes' of tumors are forming in my lungs!"

I mention this just to show you what a "tower of faith" I remained throughout this whole thing!

* * * * * * *

It is important to observe that it wasn't my towering faith that "won" me a healing. There is a real danger of putting God into a 'faith box', and assuming that anyone 'with enough faith' will be healed; and that's the only way to be healed. This thinking I believe stems from 'old line' Pentecostal teaching and was a favorite 'cop out' for evangelists who were unable to get people healed in their services. They could then pass the buck for the lack of success onto the poor, dear saints, who needed to have "edification, exhortation and comfort", rather than condemnation preached unto them.

This type of thinking falls right into line with one of Satan's master plans for preventing the people of God from receiving the healings that God would love to bestow upon them.

"Beloved, I wish above all things that thou mayest prosper and be in health, even as thy soul prospereth." (3 Jn. 2)

Satan loves to use our ignorance of God's will and Word against us. The Scripture uses two words that we usually read interchangeably, as if they were synonymous; even though they are quite different. The two words are *"Miracle"* and *"Healing"*. The former word refers to that which happens instantly; A blind eye is suddenly opened and sight instantly restored; That is a miracle. A *miracle* is that which happens in an instant; a *healing* is a cure effected over a period of time.

My *healing* from cancer was no less miraculous in the generic sense, than if it had happened in seven seconds. However, in that it did take seven months from start to finish, mine was a "healing", by Scriptural definition. What I have just stated is borne out in the words of Jesus Himself,

> Believers "shall *lay hands upon the sick . . . and they* <u>shall</u> *recover."* (MK16:17, 18)

Shall implies future action; to *recover* also implies an action taking place in the future.

It always bothers me to find some poor saint, under a weight of self-condemnation because he's either been told outright (or mistakenly believes) that the reason his healing hasn't occurred is because his faith is inadequate.

I can take no credit for what faith I do have, for "faith . . . is the gift of *God* . . . lest any man boast." (Eph. 2:8) Thus, whether God gave to me the *gift of healing,* or the *gift of faith-to-be-healed,* is really only a matter of semantics. We need only look unto Jesus Christ, the author and finisher of our faith, or unto Jesus Christ our Healer for our needs to be met!

* * * * * * *

"We cannot understand your X-Rays," the doctor continued. "That tumor of yours which we have been

93

watching all these months, just isn't there anymore! All we can find on the X-Rays is a little speck of scar tissue, on the wall of your lung where the tumor used to be!"

That evening the Lord indicated to Sue that she should get a calendar and check the timing of my healing. She did and when she checked the dates, she found that it was exactly seven months from the day when the beautiful bunch of Spirit-Baptized believers out in North Carolina had anointed me with oil and prayed for my healing, until the very day that the last X-Ray showed completely clear.

Seven is, of course, a Biblical symbol representing waiting, completion and perfection. I praise God that I wasn't healed seven months earlier, because if I had been, knowing myself as I do, I would have come to one of two possible conclusions. I would have either decided that what had happened to me was merely a 'whim' of God, or that God had set up a particular ministry in North Carolina for healing, and if I ever got sick again, I'd have to go back to North Carolina. Bless God, He, in His wisdom, led us to travel over twenty thousand miles in the intervening period, in search of healing and the power dimension of the Holy Spirit. He let us observe people being healed from coast to coast, and being Baptized in the Holy Spirit all over this nation.

If he had healed me in Kinston when we first sought prayer for healing, we would not have made this search for healing and His Truth. I would not have dug into the Scriptures as I did. We would not have made the beautiful discoveries which we have made concerning both the power and the work of the Holy Spirit.

Jesus Christ didn't heal me because I deserved it, nor because I was good, or had become sinless. He healed me for the same reasons that He healed people two thousand years ago. He was motivated then by His compassion and love for His people who were hurting. He wanted them whole, then, and He wants them whole today! Jesus Christ is still the same today! "Jesus Christ the same, yesterday, today and forever." (Heb. 13:8) He hasn't changed, He hasn't lost one iota of the power, or the love, or the compassion that He had when He walked the streets of Galilee in the flesh, now that He has ascended to sit at the right hand of God the Father! He is still a Healer, if we will but ask Him.

"Ask, and ye shall receive, that your joy may be full." (Jn. 16:24)

CHAPTER FOURTEEN.....

AFTERMATH

God is so beautifully faithful!

With Sue's consent, I began tithing in 1971 while I was disabled, and still out of work with the cancer. It seemed pretty crazy to begin tithing upon my social security disability payments, probably some of the lowest earnings I'd ever had, but that's how we began. The Scripture says:

> *"Bring ye all the tithes . . and prove me now herewith saith the Lord of Hosts, if I will not open you the windows of heaven, and pour you out a blessing, that there shall not be room enough to receive it."* (Mal. 3:10)

We gave our tithes unto the Lord *not expecting anything in return* (contrary to a lot of current teaching). However the blessings did start to roll in. I started receiving "unusual" money, from unusual, unexpected sources. I opened a special savings account at the bank for our "unusual money".

Sue and I had never been able to save much money even though I had been making fairly good money the years prior to my cancer. Whenever we had some money accumulated, we'd spend it. We probably never had more than a thousand dollars in the bank. But then the "unusual money" started coming. None of it was charity. As an example, I received the first tax refund I had ever gotten.

By the end of a year, we found that we had nearly a year's income in the bank. We felt certain that the Lord wanted us to use these funds to make available to other people, the kind of books on healing and the Baptism of the Spirit that had ministered to Sue and me. We had great difficulty obtaining such books but felt they were important.

So we started looking for a location for a retail store, and began writing to publishers for information. To our great disappointment, we were't able to find a location in our area that was suitable, for less rent than a thousand dollars a month. We felt that was way too much because we didn't know whether there would be sufficient demand for the kind of literature which we intended to carry, to even pay rent of one tenth that amount.

So, greatly disappointed after months of looking we tabled the idea of a store, and began distributing literature through book tables, at prayer meetings, and by putting racks of Christian literature in grocery and other retail stores.

During this period, Impact Books, Inc. came into being. Rod Lensch had approached my brother-in-law, Bill Bay, to reprint his testimony MY PERSONAL PENTECOST and since we had already begun purchasing books in quantity, we determined to set up Impact Books, Inc. as both a publishing house and as a mail order distribution company to distribute the healing literature.

I designed a catalog and we sent it to the printer. I was in the process of determining how to allocate the remaining funds which the Lord had provided, and invited Bill Bay to meet me for lunch. On the way to lunch, I grabbed my mail which incidentally included the printer's bill for our 10,000 catalogs. I opened the printer's bill and it was for $3,942.00. I then opened the other envelope which I'd received. It was from an insurance company. In connection with some insurance consulting work in Florida, I had been given a $100,000 life insurance policy, which also carried a disability

98

benefit. The first year's premium was covered with a note, the subsequent premiums had been paid, when due, by the disability benefit. Since I had advised the company that I would not be able to continue the policy now that I was going back to work in a virtual non-income situation, they had sent a refund check for the remaining cash value in the policy. I gasped as I read the check amount, $3,948.00!!! Enough to pay our printing bill and to cover the lunch check!

Very shortly thereafter Successful Life Bookstore began almost as miraculously. Sue and I had been offered the use of about 1000 square feet of warehouse space for the storage of our books by her parents. We had cleaned the area up and set up our warehouse and shipping room in it.

It had been nearly a year since we'd given up trying to find a retail location. Once again we began praying again for a retail location. I prayed "Lord, it seems poor stewardship for us to have 80,000 books in our warehouse, all miraculously paid-for-inventory (unheard of), and to be unable to make these books available to people locally. It would sure be nice if we could get a store on this same street, so that I could conveniently run both businesses."

This seemed a pretty good challenge even for the Lord, as there wasn't a nearby business to our knowledge that had been in business for less than about 10 years.

A week later, I was in the warehouse packing orders one Saturday morning, when Sue came in and breathlessly said, "Hey, the people who have the business next door are carrying boxes out the front door of their store and putting them in a pickup truck. Why don't you call the landlord and see what's happening?"

I did, and he told me, "I just heard about it fifteen minutes ago, myself. If you want the place, the rent is X. It's yours if you want it."

I said, "We want it."

I didn't know then how we'd be able to afford it, but I knew that if the Lord had gone to all the trouble to make it available, I'd better have the faith to take it. I checked my budget figures again and found that one company from whom I thought I would have to buy $10,000 of inventory I could get by with only buying $5,000 of inventory, which left more than enough surplus to cover the rent for the first year. We cut a hole through the wall of the warehouse into the back room of the store, and my Dad and I put in a door. So now we are able to run both businesses from one location.

I had seen God heal almost every kind of condition and work miracles, but when I saw these people go out of business, apparently in answer to prayer, it scared me! However, I needn't have worried. I later learned from the landlord, that both the husband and wife had received such good job offers, that they didn't even bother trying to sell their business. They just closed it up and sold the stock.

Making an income was not much of a factor in our thinking when we opened the bookstore. God had already worked a miracle of provision in His foresight, by having me in the insurance business for nearly 10 years. I had enough "renewal" income, that we felt we could put bread on the table and enough to keep us going on our new lower standard of living for at least three to five years, even if the store didn't make any profit at all. We opened the bookstore primarily with the intention of making available the Christian literature which had helped us, and to offer prayer and ministry for those whom the Lord might direct to us.

We didn't have to have an income, . . . God had already provided that. So if we could just sell enough books to pay the rent, or to keep the store breaking even, we'd be happy.

Needless to say, He has blessed beyond our wildest dreams. Before we ever had a book on a shelf, the Lord brought in two people who received the Baptism. One was a young man who came in off the street to offer to help me lay the carpet. It turned out that he had been seeking the Baptism in the Holy Spirit for quite a while and thought perhaps he'd had it, but had never spoken in tongues. He received! Over the course of the first year, people came and received salvation, healing, deliverance, the Baptism in the Holy Spirit, and to receive various other types of help. The Lord has continued to bring hungry people, and has continued to meet their needs.

PART II

MORE TRUTH ABOUT HEALING

"O taste and see that the Lord is good:

blessed is the man that trusteth in him."

(Psalm 34:8)

CHAPTER ONE.....

SEEK YE FIRST....

"But <u>seek</u> ye <u>first</u> the kingdom of God, and his righteousness; and all these things shall be added unto you." (Mt. 6:33)

Herein lies a key to receiving healing from the Lord! In the context of this verse, we are told that God is aware of every minute need that you and I have. We also know from His Word that He loves us with a love greater than any other we have ever known. We are His workmanship, His creation:

". . . For I am fearfully and wonderfully made:"
". . . and in thy book all my members were written, which in continuance were fashioned." (Psalm 139:14,16)

David speaks of God's awareness of us even before we were completely formed within our mothers, and he notes that God even recorded our parts. God is aware of every cell in our bodies and every hair upon our heads. He loves us and desires that we have life and have it more abundantly. However, there is a priority clearly established in God's Word: first things *first!* Seek first the Kingdom of God and His righteousness, and all these other things will fall into place. Put God first in your life: Obey Him and by obedience and submission to Him, make Him your Lord and King!

I finally came to the point in my search for healing, that having tasted the things of God and found that they were good, I became more interested in God and His Kingdom than in my healing! Obviously, if He hadn't intervened in my situation and healed me, I couldn't have lived long enough to serve Him, but serving Him, loving Him, having a good relationship with Him became of prime importance in my life.

My experience in this isn't unique: two women for whom we've prayed recently testified in a meeting that they aren't concerned any more about their healing. What they have learned about, and experienced of God so far outbalances their disease in importance that the cancer has become inconsequential to them. I have great expectation that both will shortly be as healed physically, as they have been spiritually, because they have gotten things into proper perspective: God has become of prime importance in their lives!

Having established our priorities, we need to obtain a promise from God concerning our situation. Pray and ask God to quicken to you a Scripture which covers your particular need. He might for example, if you have trouble with your feet or legs, quicken to you Psalm 116:9,

"I will walk before the Lord in the land of the living."

Our faith, if it is to exist, must be based upon what *God has promised to do* . . . not upon what man thinks! We need specific promises such as this one, to maintain our faith against the challenges that Satan will begin sending when we determine to trust God. Satan will throw attacks of pain, of fear, of doubt against you. He will attempt to cause you to doubt God; doubt His goodness; doubt the truthfulness of His Word or of His promises.

A word of caution, if you are seeking God for a healing:

don't let the negatives of the people around you get to you! You will find yourself to be surrounded by people who want you to believe their experiences (or lack of them) or their interpretation of other people's circumstances. When the "facts" seem to contradict God's Word, believe God's Word! God is True and Faithful . . . His Word is faithful and true also! If He has promised something, *its's true and it's available*!

Almost as soon as you are diagnosed as having a condition, you will probably become aware of a phenomenon which I've dubbed the "Cousin Sally Syndrome". As soon as people find out what condition you have, someone will come rushing up to tell you about *"Poor* Cousin Sally", who had exactly the same thing. They will give you all the gory details, and then tell you that in spite of her valiant battle, it finally killed her in the end. Simple strategy to combat the "Cousin Sally Syndrome": . . . *DON'T LISTEN!*

While they are talking, pray silently in the Spirit against the attack which Satan is directing against you. He is attempting to erode what faith you have.

Establish your priorities, get your Scripture, get your guard up and then dig in your heels and prepare to persevere. Your healing will probably take some time!

> *"Ask, and it shall be given you; seek, and ye shall find; knock, and it shall be opened unto you:*
> *For every one that asketh receiveth; and he that seeketh findeth; and to him that knocketh it shall be opened."* (Mt. 7:7,8)

This Scripture is a blessed promise of victory and of receiving the answer to our prayers, but it is more. It gives us a clue about persevering. The Greek tenses of the verbs give us some additional light on the truth contained here and encourages to persevere! The Greek verbs imply "ask *and keep on asking*": "seek *and keep on seeking*": and "knock *and keep on knocking*", and you shall then receive, find, and have it opened unto you.

DON'T GIVE UP . . . PERSEVERE!!!

Don't give up! You may have been trusting God for a healing for quite a while. You may feel that Satan has you on the ropes, but don't give up on God: God hasn't given up on you!

A truth that God has made very meaningful to me, is don't give up, because . . . A *DELAY* IS NOT A *NO!*

A great encouragement to perseverence for me also is the account of Daniel recorded in the tenth chapter of the Book of Daniel. In addition, it reveals some great truth about the reality of *spiritual warfare.*

Daniel had a burden for understanding the future of his people, and concerning a vision which he'd had. He had prayed about this and asked for understanding. He had backed up his prayer request with a type of a fast for twenty-one days. Then an angelic being appeared to him and spoke:

> *"Fear not, Daniel: for from the first day that thou didst set thy heart to understand, and to chasten thyself before thy god, thy words were heard, and I am come for thy words.*
> *"But the prince of the kingdom of Persia withstood me one and twenty days: but, lo, Michael, one of the chief princes came to help me."*

Consider what happened: Daniel prayed, and the *very moment* that he prayed his prayer, the answer was sent. The messenger said, in effect, the *moment that your prayer was uttered*, your *words were heard by God* and *I was dispatched*; the wheels in heaven were set in motion and I was sent from God to bring you the answer to your prayer! However, we note, this angelic messenger was restrained for three weeks by the prince of Persia. Obviously this was not an earthly prince;

for an earthly prince could not withstand a heavenly messenger. The prince of Persia mentioned, obviously refers to the satanic force or demonic prince ruling over the kingdom of Persia. Satan's forces didn't want God's message to get through. They wanted Daniel to give up in despair, or disgust, or disbelief, or frustration with God, and with his prayer unanswered. But Praise God! Daniel persisted and persevered, and the reward was his: victory resulted.

God can do anything, but His timing often isn't like ours; He often chooses to work more slowly than we would like or would expect. Thus, resulting in a testing of our faith by necessitating perseverance. If you are going to trust God for a healing . . . be prepared to wait until you receive the promise!

"And we desire that every one of you do show the same
diligence to the full assurance of hope unto the end:
That ye be not slothful, but followers of them who
through faith *and* patience *inherit the promises."*

(Heb. 6:11, 12)

CHAPTER TWO.....

IS IT GOD'S
WILL TO HEAL YOU?

Sure, he *can* heal others, *but* IS IT GOD'S WILL TO HEAL YOU? . . . OR ME? This is the question that I, as a terminal cancer patient, had to face six years ago. I found the solution to this question through the Word of God with the aid of His Spirit, and I believe that as we look together at what He showed to me, that you, too, will become convinced that IT IS INDEED THE WILL OF GOD TO HEAL *YOU!*

But first let me share with you, why it is imperative to know *what* the will of God *is* concerning *your illness.* You may say, "I know that God is able to heal; I have complete faith that He can heal me."

TO KNOW THAT GOD CAN HEAL, DOES NOT CONSTITUTE *FAITH!*

An illustration might help: I believe with all my heart that the banker around the corner *can* write me a check for $100,000.00. I do not have the slightest doubt concerning his *ability* to do it. However, I must confess to you that I have absolutely *zero faith* that he will write me such a check! Therefore, to know that someone *can do something* is not enough to create *faith* that they *will do it.* Thus, there is a missing ingredient that must be added to our knowledge of the person's *ability* to do the thing needed; we MUST also know that it is also *the will* (the desire, the intent) of that person to do the thing that we are trying to muster faith for: in this case, for our healing, WE *MUST* KNOW GOD'S WILL!

The Lord quickened this truth to me in an almost formula-like statement, "IT IS IMPOSSIBLE TO HAVE FAITH IN GOD TO DO ANYTHING THAT WE DO NOT KNOW TO BE THE WILL OF GOD!" Let that truth sink in: reread it; let God burn that into your heart, for it is a key to truth and victory in Him!

It may be easier to grasp this truth if we state it negatively: "It Is Impossible To Have Faith In God To Do Anything, That We Think God *Doesn't Want* To Do!"

It is, therefore, ESSENTIAL if faith is to exist, that you know WHAT GOD'S WILL IS, REGARDING *YOUR HEALING!*

Since the Word of God repeatedly tells us that God is no respecter of persons, we can assume that if He has promised healing for any of His children then you as a child of His are as eligible for that blessing as any other of His children. Of course I am assuming that you are a child of His: that you are in right relationship to Him through Jesus Christ. That you have confessed your need of Him; invited Jesus into your heart; and surrendered your life to Him. If you haven't yet done so, I urge you now to seek Him in His Word. See John 3:16, 17; John 1:11,12; Rev. 3:20; Acts 4:12, Acts 16:30,31; Rom. 10:8-13.

I submit to you that it is THE WILL OF GOD TO HEAL YOU for at least the following seven reasons:

I. HEALING IS A PART OF THE VERY NATURE OF GOD!

In Ex. 15:26 God, Himself, reveals His name to be Jehova-Rapha "I AM THE LORD THAT HEALETH THEE". Healing proceeds from God just as naturally as warmth radiates out from the Sun. We also see this aspect

109

of God's nature manifested in Jesus's ministry, when the woman with the flow of blood, 'but touched the hem of His garment, and was made whole instantly' . . . without Him having to pray or devote any conscious effort toward her healing. Healing just as naturally flows from His being as the warmth does from the Sun.

II. HEALING IS PROMISED BY THE COVENANT-KEEPING GOD!

In the same 26th verse quoted above, God who cannot lie, promises that "if thou wilt diligently hearken to the voice of the Lord thy God and wilt do that which is right" . . .

. . . wilt hearken to Him and wilt do what He says; and if you

. . . wilt listen to His commandments and obey all His statutes, "I WILL PUT NONE OF THESE DISEASES UPON THEE, WHICH I HAVE BROUGHT (Allowed to come) UPON THE EGYPTIANS."

God has PROMISED healing, *if* we diligently *seek Him* and *obey Him.*

III. HEALING IS AS MUCH A PART OF THE GOSPEL AS IS SALVATION.

Healing runs throughout the Bible. It first occurs in the 20th Chapter of Genesis and runs through the last pages of Revelation.

Jeremiah 17:14 "Heal me, O Lord, and I shall be healed; save me, and I shall be saved."

Psalm 103:1-3 "Bless the Lord, O my soul: and all that is within me bless His holy name. Bless the Lord, O my soul, and forget not all his benefits: Who forgiveth all thine iniquities; who *healeth all thy diseases.*"

Both Jeremiah and David recognized this dual aspect of God's plan: Salvation *and* Healing!

IV. HEALING IS IN THE ATONEMENT

When Jesus said upon the cross, "It is finished!", He meant it! Everything that needed to be done had been done. The Greek words bring out the thought: "Completely complete, and perfectly perfect." Healing was included in that complete work, and two Scriptures illustrate this clearly:

1. Mt. 8:17 "Himself took our infirmities, and bare our sicknesses." The exact same Greek work is used here for His 'bearing' of our sicknesses that is elsewhere used to describe His 'bearing' of our sins. If Jesus has borne our sins, then He has equally and with the same totality borne away our sicknesses!

2. I Peter 2:24 "Who his own self bare our sins in his own body on the tree, that we, being dead to sins, should live into righteousness: by whose stripes *ye were healed.*"

Isaiah, whom Peter here quotes, says in Isa. 53:5 "and with his stripes we are healed." Isaiah was looking forward with the mind of the Spirit, through time anticipating the work of Jesus upon the cross. While Peter looking back in time to the cross, can correctly state, "by whose stripes ye *were* healed." All that Jesus needed to do for you HAS BEEN DONE UPON THE CROSS. We must now appropriate by faith that which we need from Him.

V. THE ENTIRE EARTHLY MINISTRY OF JESUS TESTIFIES TO GOD'S WILL TO HEAL YOU!

Every person who sought healing at the hands of Jesus received it! He did not force healing upon anyone, but EVERYONE WHO *SOUGHT* HEALING at His hands RECEIVED HEALING!

Jesus was God's will manifested: "Lo, I come . . . to do *thy will,* O God." (Heb. 10:7) "My meat is to do the

111

will of him that sent me . . . " (Jn 4:34)

Matthew 12:15b, "And great multitudes followed him, and he *healed them all.*"

VI. YOU HAVE GOD'S WILL TO HEAL YOU WRITTEN WITHIN YOUR OWN BODY!

Psalm 139:14a "I am fearfully and wonderfully made . . . "

Within your own body lie obvious clues to God's will for your health and well-being. What happens when you cut your finger? The blood within your finger clots so that you do not bleed to death. The blood clots in accordance with *the will of Him who designed your body.*

When you receive a wound in your shoulder, what happens within you? Immediately your body marshalls all the necessary antibodies and dispatches them to the site of the wound. Again, in accord with *the will of Him who designed your body.* Our bodies have been designed to be "self-healing", clearly stating the will of our Great, Creator God . . . for us to BE HEALED!

Okay, you say, you're willing to accept the fact that it was God's will to heal back then, but what about today?

VII. IT IS STILL THE WILL OF GOD TO HEAL, TODAY!

We can know this quite surely: that it continues to be God's will to heal today for at least the following reasons:

1. GOD HAS SAID IT IS: III John 2 "Beloved, I wish above all things that thou mayst prosper and *be in health,* even as thy soul prospereth."

2. THE WORD SAYS IT IS: At least 30 years after the death of Jesus upon the cross, the Holy Spirit is still telling us of God's desire for His people to be well, in James 5:14: "Is any sick among you? Let him call for the elders of the church; and let

them pray over him, anointing him with oil in the name of the Lord: And the prayer of faith shall save the sick, and the Lord shall raise him up; and if he have committed sins, they shall be forgiven him. Confess your faults one to another, and pray one for another, that ye may be healed."

I had to have one final question answered: Sure God did promise healing. I could believe it for someone else, but what about me? Did He want to *heal me?*

I found that answer as I'd found all the rest, in His Word. The answer is found in the 5th chapter of Luke, in Jesus's own words!

A certain leper approached Jesus and said to him, "Lord, if thou wilt, thou canst make me clean." What the leper was really saying was, "Lord, if you *will* to do it, you could make me clean and whole of my leprosy."

Jesus answered the question of that leper, and my question when he responded with a touch of His hand and said, *"I will;* be thou clean." and the leper was immediately made clean.

Jesus, in essence, said to the leper (and to me, and to you): "I *DO* WILL IT, IT IS MY WILL ... MY DESIRE ... MY INTENT ... BE THOU WHOLE!"

PART III

MORE TRUTH ABOUT
THE BAPTISM
IN THE HOLY SPIRIT

"I send the promise of the Father upon you."

(Lk 24:49)

CHAPTER ONE.....

ARE TONGUES FOR EVERYONE?

When we first began to pray for people to receive the Baptism in the Holy Spirit, I believed that some would receive it with tongues, some without tongues, some would get tongues later, and some would never get tongues. Not too surprisingly, that's exactly what we saw happen: some got it with tongues, some got tongues later, some never got tongues so far as we know.

In every instance in Scripture, however, where the Baptism in the Holy Spirit is recorded as occuring, a *supernatural sign* and *seal* of that Baptism was given to *each* recipient; not to prove something to someone else, but to let *each of them* know that they had indeed been Baptised. The Lord very graciously showed me several years ago through two very unique and dramatic examples that tongues *are a part of the Baptism* and that they *are for every believer* who is willing to receive them!

CHAPTER TWO.....

TONGUES FOR A DOZEN NEAR SCOTT A. F. B.

Although we had a real desire to serve the Lord, we had determined not to get ahead of Him, and that we were going to wait for Him to open the doors. I wanted to share the story of what He had done for me, but I *vowed never to ask to speak: to wait to be invited.* The Lord is so beautifully faithful: He began opening doors for us to give our testimony to churches, church groups, Bible study and home prayer groups, and FGBMFI chapter meetings around the country. Sometimes as many as thirty to fifty church groups in a year, and nearly as many FGBMFI meetings.

An early meeting that built my confidence was one at Scott Air Force Base in Belleville, Illinois. I had shared my testimony with the group and had offered to pray for healing, and then afterwards offered to pray with anyone desiring the Baptism in the Holy Spirit. Col. Doug Brewer, the Chaplain, suggested, when I asked for a place with more privacy than the main meeting room, that we move over into their prayer room. I suggested to Doug that he might minister concerning the Baptism to the candidates, but he very graciously deferred, stating that he felt "the anointing was on me."

I directed those desiring the Baptism to bring their chairs out to the center of the room. I think there were about five or six who wanted the Baptism, but there was also a crowd of people ringing the room. I asked Doug about them, and he explained, "They have already received. They just want to watch you minister the Baptism, so they can learn how to do it."

What he didn't realize, and I didn't quite know how to tell him, was that *I didn't know how either!* I had at that time only prayed for a very few people to receive. However, since he felt that I was "anointed", that was good enough for me. It built my confidence and besides, *my God could do anything!*

I explained the Baptism to the candidates, then answered their questions about it, and prayed for them to be Baptised in the Holy Spirit. The Lord Baptised them all and *they all began to speak in tongues.* Suddenly though, something else interesting happened. People in the spectator's circle began to cry. The Holy Spirit was falling upon several people who thought they had already been Baptised in the Spirit, but had never spoken in tongues. Some of the onlookers apparently hadn't really been Baptised, and some, it turned out, were just there out of curiosity. In any event, the Lord Baptised about seven more with the Holy Spirit. It seemed that as soon as one received, someone else across the room would be touched and begin to cry and they too would then receive. Some even received before we could pray with them.

This was one of the experiences wherein the Lord went beyond our expectations and began to show us *that He desired those who received the Baptism in the Holy Spirit to be able to pray in the Spirit!* The second example was even more dramatic. It occurred near Chicago and it caught me even more by surprise. It began this way . . . .

CHAPTER THREE.....

TONGUES FOR
FIFTY NEAR CHICAGO

Very shortly after our return to St. Louis from Georgia, we were invited to attend a prayer meeting in Valley Park, a suburb of St. Louis about 15 miles from our home. We learned that the meetings were being held in Rodney Lensch's basement. We arrived at the meeting and after it began with a few hymns, Rod recognized us and asked if we'd like to share about our experiences on our trip or about my healing. (I guess he could see the improvement.)

I shared that evening about the miracles that we'd seen in Georgia and about my healing. I shared up to the point of having lived through the six things that were to have killed me. I could not say that the tumor was gone from my lung because it was still there. Nevertheless, I told them that I was finally convinced that God *was healing* me and that I believed that He would take the tumor also.

Unbeknownst to me, a beautiful Franciscian nun whom Sue and I have since learned to know and love, was in the back row recording on her cassette tape recorder the things that I said. Through a miraculous series of events, the tape she made that night found its way to a Lutheran pastor in Chicago with whom I'd gone all through school and college. He called me several days later, relating that he had heard the tape and asking if he and his wife could come and visit with us.

After I had retold my story to them in person, he summed up by saying, "Well, Bill, I know you were a nut before, and you're still the same kind of nut, but I can see that you have had a valid spiritual experience! If I can get my church council to go along with it, would you and Sue be willing to come to Chicago and share your story with my whole congregation?"

I agreed with a slight butterfly feeling in my stomach, as I had never spoken to a large group before and didn't feel adequate.

Months later the invitation came. Sue and I and our boys climbed into a borrowed camper and headed for Chicago, feeling like 'evangelists hitting the trail.'

The first night we spoke in their church, we gave our testimony and then prayed for healing and saw approximately thirty to sixty people healed. About 1:30 that morning the minister and his wife received the Baptism in the Holy Spirit and both spoke in tongues. The next morning on the way to church for the morning service, he announced to me, "Bill, I want you to tell my people about the Baptism in the Holy Spirit tonight in the evening service. I want you to tell them *the whole truth; tongues and everything!* Don't hold anything back! This is too good for any of them to miss. I don't care if it costs me my church. I don't want any of them to miss it."

I didn't know what to talk about. So I sat down after church, with my Bible and began listing the Scriptures which related to the Baptism in the Holy Spirit.

That evening after I had shared the Scriptures and some personal observations with the people present, I gave my "faith-filled" altar-call which consisted of, "I'm going to go get a drink of water. When I come back, if there are any of you who'd like to receive the Baptism of the Holy Spirit, we'll pray with you: Also if there are any who wish prayer for healing, we'll pray for them. I'd like those who want the

119

Baptism to come sit on the front rows of the left side of the church, and those desiring healing to sit on the right front side."

I then went to the lobby for a drink of water and to give those who wanted to leave a chance to depart. After a few minutes I returned to the sanctuary of the church and was amazed to see that it appeared as if no one had moved. There were about 50 people sitting in the left front section. I returned to the platform and motioned for the minister to join me. When he did, I said, "Hey, they must have misunderstood me. There *can't* be that many wanting the Baptism in the Holy Spirit." (I had told him before the service that there probably wouldn't be more than one or two people who would want the Baptism and that we would pray for them first, so as to have that additional prayer power when we proceeded to pray for the healings.)

He replied, "Sure, you're right. I'll take care of it."

He then announced to the congregation, "I think you all didn't quite understand Bill. We want those who want the Baptism to sit here on the left front pews and those who want healing on the right front."

At that point a minister in the back queried loudly, "Where do we go if we want both?"

"We are going to pray for the Baptism first." The minister stated.

Whereupon another whole crowd of people got up and moved over into the left side of the church.

I began a quick but earnest conversation with the Lord, "Lord, you know that I don't have the slightest idea how to pray for this many people. There must be over seventy people out there, and I've never prayed for more than about five at a time to receive the Baptism, and I thought that was too many. I prefer to pray for one at a time so I can answer their questions.

"I am not the One who Baptises, though, Lord. You are

the Baptiser, and you are going to have to do whatever gets done. I really only know how to pray for one at a time, so I'm going to say the same prayer that I'd say for one person, and you'll have to do whatever else needs to be done."

So I then prayed for them, realizing that once again the Lord had gotten me into a situation where I had to trust Him entirely; and where I knew that *I* was in over *my* head. When I completed the prayer, I began laying my hands on two people at a time in the front row. They immediately began to speak in tongues! As soon as they did, I moved to the next two. The six in the front pew all praying in tongues, I moved to the second pew, with the same results. By the time I reached the third pew, the minister joined in laying on hands in the next row. The candidates upon whom he laid his hands had the same thing happen: they too began to speak in tongues.

Sue returned at about that time and she joined us. (She explained to me later, "I saw that mob of people, and I knew that I didn't have the faith for this. So I went to read the pamphlets in the lobby.")

To my joy! To the thrill of my heart and to the *confirmation of His word,* Jesus baptized every person there who was open to receiving the Baptism. (Some refused to let us pray for them when we got to them, and some got up and left before we got to them: apparently just being there as observers or on-lookers; sitting in to see if anything would actually happen.) Everyone willing to receive, received the Baptism: and *all* of them, *over fifty in number, received* and they *all spoke in tongues!*

I was amazed, thrilled and strengthened by what I witnessed occur in that Lutheran Church. I later realized that God certainly didn't love Lutherans in Chicago any more than He loved Catholics, Baptists or Presbyterians in St. Louis (or anywhere else), and that *what He had done for them He would do for others.* He is no respecter of persons;

therefore all are equally eligible for the *same confirmation* of *their Baptism.*

In light of this experience in Chicago, God convinced me that tongues were indeed a part of the Baptism and indeed for all! As a result of His having worked this truth deeply into my heart, I haven't seen anyone in the past *five years* Baptized in the Holy Spirit without their also receiving, *at the same time,* a new personal, private devotional language!

Now I should point out that there is no particular power in me other than the TRUTH of His word, confirmed by Him to my heart. Perhaps I am willing to spend more time with a person seeking the Baptism, than others might, because I *know* that *God is going to give them a language!* Many people ministering who aren't so sure, will pray and if the language doesn't come pretty quickly, they say "Well, go on home, you'll get it in your car on the way home, or when you make the bed, or the next time you get in *a tub of hot water.* Thus, we can see the grain of truth, experientially, upon which the rumors or experiences are based. Unfortunately some of the big names ministering today are guilty of what I consider to be sloppy ministry in this area. I have heard a number of them wind up their ministry for the Baptism with, "Well, most of you have already spoken in tongues, the rest of you will get it later. I have to leave now to catch my plane."

Tragically those who haven't yet received, by the time the minister "has to leave" will leave the meeting feeling that tongues weren't meant for them, or somehow as if they are "second-class" Christians, and they'll probably go out like many others and write books trying to prove that tongues *aren't* for everybody. I have had many occasions to minister to these "once burned-twice shy" candidates for the Baptism, who often aren't willing to risk failing to receive again for several years. Those who minister need to "establish their hearts," that they might know *the Lord's will* and *perform it* in this area.

CHAPTER FOUR.....

EASIER TO RECEIVE
THAN WE'D IMAGINE

It's really very simple to receive the Baptism in the Holy Spirit: so easy, that I almost received it as a child before I'd ever heard of anyone receiving in modern times. When I was seven years old, I was given a Bible for Christmas by my Grandmother. I determined as an 'act of faith' that I was going to read the whole Bible or at least the New Testament. I dutifully read the four gospels, the Book of Acts, and then ran into Paul's writing and gave up in utter frustration. However something very interesting happened, which I had completely forgotten about, until just recently when a middle-aged woman related an experience very similar to my own.

As I was reading the books of Acts, I was deeply touched in my seven year old heart, by the accounts of the disciples being Baptized in the Holy Spirit, and speaking in tongues. Since I was then unencumbered with 'theological hangups', and was able to merely accept what I read as truth, I didn't doubt it at all: I believed what the Bible said.

Since the Baptism seemed to be so natural a part of the believers role, and so significant a part (Jesus Himself *commanding* the disciples not to leave Jerusalem without receiving it Acts 1:4) of the equipping of the disciples, I determined to ask for it.

I was laying in my bed reading the Bible by the light of one of those bullet-shaped bed lamps so common in the forties. I put my face down on the sheet and prayed "Lord, Jesus, you baptized your followers, the 120 in the upper room, and others with your Holy Spirit. I believe that you can still do that and I just ask you now to Baptize me with your Holy Spirit."

When I found that I didn't hear the sound of the mighty rushing wind or feel tongues of fire descending upon me or whatever other kind of experience I was expecting, I continued my prayer. "Lord, I am going to trust you right now to give me a new language just like you gave to them. I am going to bring up sounds and offer my voice up to you. You take the sounds of my mouth and make them into the language that you want me to speak."

I then began bringing up sounds, and began speaking words that I couldn't understand. I am sure now, looking back, that I was *beginning to speak in tongues* . . . I believe that had I continued, the Lord would have completed my Baptism right then.

However, like many another earnest Christian, I let the enemy take advantage of my uncertainty (doubt). He planted doubts and I accepted them. "That's you speaking." "You're making it up." "You're talking baby-talk." "It's not really tongues."

Since I believed Satan's lies rather than the Word of God, I assumed that God didn't want to answer my prayer, and that tongues weren't for me. I then promptly forgot about it for almost thirty years until I heard a very similar testimony, from a woman who hadn't given up so easily as I had. She received the Baptism as a little child when she asked, and has been using her language ever since.

CHAPTER FIVE.....

TONGUES ARE A
"DŌRON"

You will recall that the Greek word we mentioned earlier for *Gift* is *"Dōron"*. This word is the one used throughout the New Testament whenever reference is made to God's *gift* to us of Christ, to the *gift* of salvation, to the *gift* of eternal life, or to the *gift* of the Holy Spirit. In the book of Acts, where we find the only recorded accounts of people receiving the Baptism, the word most associated with the Charismatic movement, "Charisma" or "Charismata", is not used, even once, in reference to the Baptism or the attendant languages spoken!

In every instance in the Book of Acts the word *gift* is translated from the root word *"Dōron"*. Especially interesting for us are the references in Acts 10 and 11, where Peter makes reference to the people at the house of Cornelius receiving the like *gift* (including the manifestation of tongues) as the disciples and apostles had at Pentecost.

The Lord has convinced me that the *"Dōron"* of the Spirit, includes *one* kind of tongues!

There are *two* kinds of tongues in the Scripture. Most people do not recognize this truth, and I would estimate that ninety-five percent of the confusion over tongues stems from this misunderstanding. It is, for example, impossible to understand correctly the 14th chapter of First Corinthians, no matter how many degrees a person may have, without this one underlying truth.

The first kind of tongues, is that which is given, or available, the moment one is Baptized with the Holy Spirit. It is a personal, private devotional language. This is that which is defined by Paul in 1 Cor. 14:2.

"He that speaketh in an unknown tongue speaketh not unto men, but unto God; for no man understandeth him."

(emphasis ours) Clearly this is that personal, private devotional language, directed to God, and intended for your prayer closet: To be used in private because *man cannot understand it!*

The other kind of tongues is the "gift of tongues", found in the listing of the nine "gifts" of the Spirit in I Cor. 12:8-10. Gift number eight in the listing is the gift of "divers kinds of tongues" or a *different* kind of tongues. This kind of tongues is followed in the listing by gift number nine, "the interpretation of tongues". It is also followed *in practice* by interpretation.

This is the kind of tongues one may hear in a public gathering or assembly, or meeting. Someone speaks a message in tongues audibly in public; it is then followed by an interpretation in English. This is *God speaking*, in tongues a 'message' to the people present. He speaks the message through the mouth of someone present, in tongues. He then speaks the interpretation of that "message" through the same mouth, or the mouth of someone else present . . . but the second time it is spoken in the native tongue, or language, of the people present.

The important thing for us to recognize here is primarily the matter of *direction;* the first kind of tongues (personal, private devotional language) is directed vertically *toward God* (I Cor. 14:2), the latter, public ministry kind of tongues, is directed toward man (I Cor. 12:10). The former is *man*

126

speaking to God, the latter is *God speaking to man!*

The message spoken and interpreted will have the same purpose as prophesying (I Cor. 14:5, tongues with interpretation) "edification, exhortation and comfort." (I Cor. 14:3).

Paul is far too logical, and the Holy Spirit far too intelligent for the obvious apparent contradiction concerning tongues to exist, that is usually cited. Paul is far too logical to say on the one hand, "Do all speak with tongues?" (I Cor. 12:30) in the Greek expecting an obvious negative answer; And on the other hand, "I would" (or I Pray) "that ye all spake in tongues!" (I Cor. 14:5).

Since we know that the Scripture cannot contradict itself, the mistake must lie in our understanding. The apparent contradiction is not a contradiction at all, when we see it in the light of this Truth. All believers can, indeed, pray in a personal, private devotional language (as is needful *for personal edification* I Cor. 14:4). However all believers cannot speak in tongues publicly, if we are going to follow prescribed Scriptural order:

"If any man speak in an unknown tongue, let it be by two or at the most by three, and that by course; and let one interpret."

(I Cor. 14:27)

This tells us that if someone is going to speak in tongues in the assembly (vs. 26 "when ye come together") it is to be *done one at a time* and there *is to be an interpretation.* As I read the Scripture, this indicates that there isn't to be speaking in tongues publicly by a lot of people, lest *unbelievers* come in, or those believers *"unlearned"* in the ways of the Spirit who will be convinced that the speakers are *"mad".* (I Cor. 14:23).

Paul is very careful in the 14th Chapter of First Corinthians, to differentiate between the two kinds of tongues, and the settings where each kind is appropriate. He makes it very clear when he is speaking of the public ministry tongues used in a public setting ("edifying of the church," "in the church", "the whole church be come together," "when ye come together"). He also indicates when the one speaking in tongues is to do it privately (for example vs 2; vs 18, 19, & 28).

He closes with an admonition that is apparently all too often overlooked by many Christians today, *"Forbid not to speak with tongues."* (I Cor. 14:39).

CHAPTER SIX.....

HOW TO RECEIVE
THE BAPTISM
IN THE HOLY SPIRIT

God is sovereign and can move in any manner He chooses; so I am not offering a rigid formula but rather some suggestions.

PREPARATION:

Step I. I would suggest that you begin by praying for the Lord to open the truth of the Baptism in the Holy Spirit to you, and to give you a real hunger for it.

Step II. If you have not read John Sherrill's *They Speak With Other Tongues,* you might find it helpful, although it certainly isn't a prerequisite.

At Cornelius's house in Acts 10, the candidates hadn't read any books on the subject; hadn't memorized any Scriptures; nor worked at cleaning themselves up: their only qualification was that they had hearts hungering for more of what God had for them. They heard their very first sermon, accepted the salvation message presented them by Peter , apparently before Peter even considered them ready for an altar-call, the Lord Jesus Baptised them with the Holy Spirit!

Peter and the others with him, knew that they had indeed received the Baptism,

> *"For they heard them speak with tongues and magnify God."*
> (Acts 20:46)

Their desire to receive what God had for them, apparently made them eligible!

Step III. Read or reread the accounts in the Book of Acts where the Baptism occurred. (Acts. 2,8,9,10,19) Resolve in your mind that tongues are included, so that you know what you are asking for, and how you will know when you have received it.

Step IV. Now, prayerfully and with expectation in your heart to receive go on to the next section.

INTRODUCTION TO THE BAPTISER

Jesus gives us at least three witnesses unto Himself as the one who Baptises with the Holy Spirit. The first witness is *John the Baptist.* In Matthew 3:11, he announces:

> *"I indeed, baptize you with water unto repentance but he who cometh after me is mightier than I, whose shoes I am not worthy to bear; he shall baptize you with the Holy Spirit and with fire."*

Then Jesus came to the Jordan to be baptized by John, and John attempted to forbid Him, saying:

> *"I have need to be baptized of thee and comest thou to me?"*

In other words, John was saying, I need to be baptized by you with the Holy Spirit and do you come to me to be baptized in water? However, Jesus told him to go ahead and baptize Him with water to fulfill all righteousness; and he did:

"And Jesus when he was baptized went up straightaway out of the water; and, lo, the heavens were opened unto him and he (John) saw the Spirit of God descending like a dove and lighting upon him: And lo, a voice from heaven saying, this is my beloved Son, in whom I am well pleased."

John gives that same testimony of Jesus in each of the first three Gospels.

The second witness to Jesus as the one who baptizes with the Holy Spirit, is *God the Father!* In the beginning of the Book of John, John the Baptist again is speaking, and he says:

"I baptize with water; but there standeth one among you, whom ye know not; He it is, who coming after me is preferred before me, whose shoe's latchet I am not worthy to unloose."
Then he saw Jesus coming again and he said,
"Behold the Lamb of God, which taketh away the sin of the world."
And then John bore witness saying,
"I saw the Spirit descending from heaven like a dove, and it abode upon him. And I knew him not: but <u>he</u> that sent me to baptize with water, <u>the same</u> said unto me, 'Upon whom thou shalt see the Spirit descending, and remaining on him the same is He which baptises with the Holy Ghost!' And I saw and bare record that this is the Son of God."

The third witness that we find is *Jesus*, Himself. In the Book of Luke (24:49), He says:

"Behold I send the promise of my Father upon you; but tarry ye in the city of Jerusalem, until ye be endued with power from on high."

He repeats that promise again in the Book of Acts, when He doesn't suggest or recommend that His followers be baptised with the Holy Spirit: He rather, "*commanded them that they should not depart from Jerusalem, but wait for the* promise of the Father, which, saith He, ye have heard of me. For John truly baptized with water; but ye shall be baptized with the Holy Ghost not many days hence."

And in the 8th verse:

"But ye shall receive power after that the Holy Ghost is come upon you; and ye shall be witnesses unto me both in Jerusalem, and in all Judea, and in Samaria and unto the uttermost part of the earth."

Herein we can see three great truths: First, it is *Jesus Christ Himself who is going to baptise you* with the Holy Spirit: not any man, or any denomination. It is *Jesus* that will give you a supernatural *sign* and *seal* of your baptism, not to prove something to someone else, but to let *you* know, beyond any shadow of a doubt, that he has Baptised you with the Holy Spirit! He will give you a new language; a personal, private devotional language, or let you pray in tongues!

Second, it is a *Baptism of power*: power to live the kind of lives we've been called to live, and cannot generate within ourselves.

Third, it is *power for a purpose:* the purpose being to become more effective witnesses for Him: working in partnership with the Holy Spirit. The Holy Spirit going before us to prepare the hearts to which we will speak: the Holy Spirit guiding and directing our words to reach the needs of those hearts!

The Scriptures as we have just seen, clearly present Jesus as the One who Baptises with the Holy Spirit!

Now, let me share just a few thoughts with you that may be helpful. We all want the Baptism; we all want the power; we all want the love, joy, and peace — the fruit of the Spirit. However the thing that we usually don't want, is the tongues! The tongues are a stumbling block for us, for any of a number of reasons. The enemy's chief weapons against us are

132

fear and doubt. He uses these with regard to tongues too. He hits us with *fear of the unknown;* tongues are an *unknown* to us. He hits us with *fear of abuses and misuses* that we may have heard of concerning tongues. He uses a great many things: possibly even the *fear that it wouldn't happen to us,* to attempt to prevent our receiving all the blessings that God has for us.

Yet we know that it *cannot* be that hard to receive, when we consider the people who have previously received the Baptism and spoken in tongues: the 120 at Pentecost, and the group at the House of Cornelius who hadn't prepared themselves in any way. It can't be that difficult. Part of the problem people often have is that they feel that they *must understand* all about tongues in order to receive. By definition tongues are a supernatural language — a miracle language — they are beyond our ability to understand. We cannot understand tongues! Another part of our problem stems from the fact that we haven't understood *how God works miracles.* We've always thought, "God, if you're going to work a miracle, I'll praise you for it, but I don't want to get involved."

God, in His wisdom, has chosen to involve man in miracles! Man does the natural; God does the supernatural! God *could have parted* the Red Sea without any help from Moses, *but He chose to have Moses play a part!* Moses did the natural; God did the supernatural. The same truth is illustrated by Peter in walking upon the water. In a way, we also see a foreshadowing of some truth about the Baptism in the Holy Spirit and speaking in tongues. There wasn't anything miraculous about the manner in which Peter got out of his boat. There wasn't anything miraculous about the way Peter began to walk, because Peter got out of the boat and began to walk the same way he did at the end of everyday's fishing, when he pulled his boat up on dry land. It wasn't until Peter got out of his boat, the way he always did, and began to walk the way he always did, that God *could do the supernatural and sustain him* so that he didn't sink into the waves. God *could not do the miraculous part until Peter had done the natural:* Peter had to do the natural *before* God could do the supernatural! The same thing is true of the Baptism in the Holy Spirit and speaking in tongues. We too, *must do the natural* before God can do the *supernatural!*

Many people seem to make the mistake that I made when I was first prayed for to receive the Baptism. I sat there with my mouth shut, just waiting for God to grab my jaws, wiggle my tongue and to make noises come out of my mouth. I was waiting for Him *to force me to speak in tongues.* God *will not force anyone to speak in tongues!* If He were going to force us to speak in tongues, we would all have been speaking in tongues for a long time! So He obviously isn't going to force us!

Since we see that God isn't going to *make us* speak in tongues against our will, then we must make a decision (or some decisions) in order to receive the Baptism and to speak in tongues. When Jesus said that believers . . . "shall speak with new tongues," (Mk 16:17) He doesn't mean new vocal organs: He is talking about *language.* He is referring to *tongue* in the sense of the Hebrew *tongue* or the Aramaic *tongue*: He means language.

The speaking of that language isn't miraculous: it is *that which is spoken* that is miraculous! Your same old mouth, larynx, breath, teeth, tongue and lips will be involved in the speaking of it: that which is spoken is the miraculous part!

As we have said, there are some decisions to be made in order to receive. I think we can boil them down to three.

The first decision is *to ask for it!* The Scripture says in Luke 11:13, "If ye then, being evil, know how to give good gifts unto your children, how much more shall your heavenly Father give the Holy Spirit to them that ask him?" *Asking* is a condition for receiving the Baptism.

The second decision we must make is the decision *to stop speaking in English*. We cannot speak two natural languages at the same time. For example, I cannot speak now in what little Spanish, Greek, or Latin that I know as long as I am speaking in English!

The third decision that we have to make is the decision *to speak!* You must decide to take a deep breath; to bring up a sound and offer it up to the Lord, trusting Him to be able to form that sound into a word that is pleasing unto His ear. For example, I could be the most eloquent man on earth, and yet, if I sat facing you with my mouth shut, you wouldn't know for sure but what I was a mute!

Now those are the three decisions that you must make. Do you still want to receive the Baptism in the Holy Spirit? If so, do you wish to seriously enough to make these three decisions?

If you do, . . . Let us pray:

"Lord Jesus, I thank you for this servant of yours, whom you have called and to whom you have given a hunger for more of You. I pray now that you will Baptise this child of yours with the Holy Spirit and grant a release in a new personal, private, devotional language with which to praise your Holy Name! I thank you for it in Jesus' Name!"

Now, you ask the Lord in English to Baptise you with the Holy Spirit.

Stop praying in English!

Relax and drink Him in!

Now, you love Jesus, and Jesus loves you. There isn't a sound that you can make that will be displeasing unto Him. Trust Him enough to take a deep breath, to bring up a sound and to offer it up to Him; trusting Him to make it into a word that is pleasing unto His ear. Just make the decision right now, to tell Jesus that you love Him . . . without saying it in English, or any other language that you know. Love Him

135

with the sounds from your heart. Let the sounds of your heart, speak to Him your love for Him.

Just keep on bringing up sounds of love for Him.

CHAPTER SEVEN.....

NOW THAT YOU HAVE RECEIVED THE BAPTISM

Now there are a few things that I would like to share with you, just as I do with each person with whom I pray personally. Even if you aren't completely sure that you have received, if you have prayed and uttered sounds that you didn't understand, read on!

Praise God! You have just been Baptised in the Holy Spirit! You may have felt it very deeply, or you may feel that you have merely performed an act of obedience. Nevertheless, you have received the Baptism in the Holy Spirit, and the Lord has given to you the same *sign* and *seal* of your Baptism that He has given to believers from the beginning: He has given you a new language! Just as you have previously had the "tool" of *praying in English,* so too, you now have the "tool" of *praying in the Spirit,* or praying *in tongues.*

There are a number of reasons why you should *continue* to pray in tongues now that you have once begun. Paul tells us in I Cor. 14:4 that,

"He that speaketh in an unknown tongue edifieth himself."

Your spirit is *edified* or *built up* when you "pray in the Spirit." The Greek word implies, having your spirit *charged*

137

up in the same sense that a battery is charged. Also over in Ephesians chapter six, where Paul speaks of putting on "the whole armour of God": the last element of that armour which is almost always overlooked, is "praying in the Spirit." In Jude 20, we are told that our *faith is built up* when we pray "in the Holy Ghost" (Holy Spirit)!

There are many references to continuing to pray in the Spirit, let me share two of the most important reasons. Paul in Romans 8:26 tells us that we don't know how to pray as we ought. Any prayer that you or I would pray right now, in English, would be a prejudiced and biased prayer. It would be prejudiced by the needs that we are aware of, and biased by the people whom we love. This very moment the greatest need in the mind of the Spirit might be someone across town in a hardware store having a heart attack. We couldn't be aware of that need with our minds, but as we yield ourselves to the Spirit, the Spirit can then *help our infirmity* and *pray through us a perfect prayer, in accordance with the will of God, making intercession for the needs of the saints.*

Finally, I think we find the highest calling both to the Baptism in the Holy Spirit and to continuing to pray in the Spirit, in the answer of Jesus to the woman at the well: "The hour is coming and now is, when the true worshippers shall worship the Father in spirit and in truth: for the Father seeketh such to worship him. God is a Spirit: and they that worship him must worship him in spirit and in truth." (Jn 4:23,24)

Until the Spiritual 'scales' fell from my eyes, I thought that this passage referred to the spirit of the law and the letter of the law. Then I saw the truth: He is referring to *praying* (worshipping) *in the Spirit!* What a fantastic thought: that God Almighty, the Creator of the universe, has a desire in His heart that you and I can now fill! We can now *worship Him in the Spirit* . . . for the Father *seeketh such* to worship Him!

You cannot, of course, feel your spirit, so you will not feel it being edified or built up. Nevertheless, the Word of God tells us that in the unseen realm of the Spirit, our spirits are being strengthened. This is a situation much like my right arm. God has given to me the gift of a good right arm. I with my mind, can make a decision not to use it, and it will hang lifelessly at my side. It is still, nonetheless, the gift of a good right arm, but I have chosen not to use it. On the other hand, I can make the decision to use my right arm: exercise it: become more skilled in its use. It can then do for me all the things that it was intended to do. So too, with the good gift of tongues that the Lord has given to you. The more you use it, the more that it can do for you!

Remember, the Lord doesn't force you to pray in English: *you* have to *make the decision* to pray in English today, or else *you* won't pray in English today. So too, *you* will have to make the decision to pray in the Spirit.

You will find that you can now pray in the Spirit without moving your lips. Just as you could right now, pray the Lord's prayer without moving your lips; so too, you can pray in the Spirit *silently*, without moving your lips, or disturbing anyone around you. You can also sing in the Spirit. (I Cor. 14:15) It is your decision to make, as to how you are going to pray. For example, who determines whether you pray loudly or softly in English? Rapidly or slowly? Whether you sing or speak your prayer? You do, of course! You are now going to have to make all those same decisions concerning the way that you will pray in tongues.

Now you must do your part: make the decision to use and become more skilled in this new gift that God in His wisdom has chosen to give to you!

One final thought that I always share with people before they leave is this; "Before you can get through the nearest doorway, Satan is going to try to put a "Harpie" on your shoulder, if he hasn't already, to try to take the Baptism in the Holy Spirit away from you! He can't steal the Baptism from you, but you need some truth to keep you free:

First: *Satan and every demon in Hell could not prevent Jesus Christ — the Baptiser — from Baptising you with the Holy Spirit!* They may have delayed it, but they couldn't prevent it!

Second, *Satan and every demon in Hell cannot take away from you that which Jesus Christ has given to you!* They aren't that big and they aren't that strong!

Since they know these two truths even better than we do, and since they also know how much *power* is generated when a Christian prays in the Spirit, they are going to do everything in their power to try to keep you and me from praying in the Spirit! The chief weapon that they will attempt to use against you, will be the "Harpie" which we just mentioned. It is going to whisper lies of fear and doubt into your ear. These lies will sound like the following examples: "That couldn't have been the Baptism in the Holy Spirit because it didn't feel like it!" or . . . "Because you don't deserve it!": because "You are still a sinner!" "Remember this sin or that one!"; or that couldn't have been the Baptism . . . "because the Lord couldn't have loved *you* like He loved Peter, Paul and John — you're not in their league! Who do you think you are?"

You may never have heard tongues in your life, but Satan will instantly make you an *expert* on tongues: "That doesn't sound like tongues to me!" "Those sounds you are uttering aren't tongues!" "That can't be tongues because it doesn't *feel* like tongues!" "It's not tongues — it's babytalk!" "It's jibberish!" "You are just being emotional!" "It's from the devil!" "It's nonsense syllables!" "You're making it up!" "You're repeating sounds that you've heard someone else say!" "It isn't really a language!"

There you have more than a dozen of the chief types of doubts that Satan may throw at people who have received.

140

We can put the lie to Satan on most of them right here and now! First of all, if you heard the words (or sounds) in your mind, or felt them in your heart or throat or mouth, before you spoke them, that's fine! You got them from the right source; you didn't get them from me! Neither I nor anyone else prayed in tongues with you before you began to pray in tongues. I never pray in tongues with anyone seeking the Baptism until after they themselves have begun to pray in the Spirit: for the very reason that I don't want them thinking that they got their language from me! Yours is real, even if it may not seem to sound the way you expected!

Now before you go, let's just thank the Lord for Baptising you with the Holy Spirit; and let's thank Him, *in the new language* that *He has given you.* You will start yourself now, just as you did before: just take a deep breath, and tell Jesus that you love Him ... but don't say it in English!

"Pray without ceasing." (I Thess. 5:17)

If the truths concerning healing contained in this book have been helpful and enlightening to you, then you will want to obtain all or some of the following tapes of teaching on healing by the same author. These tapes contain simple, clear, logical, Scriptural teaching and explanations of the healing ministry. Each tapes is $4.95, or the complete set is just $59.40.

1. INTRODUCTION TO THE HEALING MINISTRY
2. OVERCOMING BLOCKS TO HEALING
3. IS HEALING FOR EVERYONE?
4. WHAT IF HEALING HASN'T HAPPENED (YET)?
5. HEALING IS FOR THE BODY!
6. CONDITIONS FOR ANSWERED PRAYER FOR HEALING
7. THREE KINDS OF FAITH FOR HEALING
8. HEALING IS THE CHILDREN'S BREAD
9. PERSEVERANCE OF DANIEL
10. HAST THOU CONSIDERED JOB -PART I
11. HAST THOU CONSIDERED JOB -PART 11
12. HOW TO MINISTER TO THE SICK
13. DIVINE HEALTH/HEALING AND ANSWERS ·
14. NEW FACTORS, NEW WAYS TO RECEIVE HEALING

All of the books mentioned in *Alive Again!* are available through **Impact Christian Books, Inc.**

They Speak With Other Tongues	p. 8.99
The Cross and The Switchblade	p. 8.99
I Believe in Miracles	p. 9.99
The Will of God	p. 5.00

(Prices subject to change)

Write For Our Catalog Listing Over 600 Bestselling Paperback Titles.
IMPACT CHRISTIAN BOOKS, INC.,
332 Leffingwell Ave., Kirkwood, Mo. 63122.

Or, visit our website:*www.impactchristianbooks.com*
FOR AN AMAZING SELECTION OF POWERFUL CHRISTIAN BOOKS

AMAZING ANSWERS ABOUT HEALING...

THREE KINDS OF FAITH FOR HEALING

Many today have been taught that the only way to be healed is to personally have faith for their healing. It is implied, one must somehow 'work up' or develop enough personal *faith-to-be-healed,* and then healing will come. Many have also been told that the reason they remain afflicted is because of their lack of faith.

Such statements in addition to being utterly devoid of compassion, are terribly devastating to the poor hearers. One could never imagine Jesus saying something so heartless. Yet these things are often said today. Even those who have not heard these words spoken aloud have received them through implication from proud, spiritually 'superior' friends who believe that these sick individuals are somehow deficient in faith.

There is good news both for them and for us, because that teaching is wrong. There are more ways of being healed than just the one way, as we have been taught.

In this new book, Bill Banks presents a *revelation* of three main types of faith for healing illustrated in Scripture, and a fourth which is a combination of the other three.

Three Kinds of Faith For Healing   **Paper 4.95**

Powerful Help on Cassette

Are You Saved? Have You Been BORN AGAIN? Do you even know for sure what is meant by these questions?

If not, we strongly recommend that you send for the tape
   HOW TO BE SAVED, or BORN AGAIN!

To receive this informative tape, which can change your life . . . just as it has for thousands of others, when they have heard the message contained on the tapes and responded to it. . . .

   Simply send your name and address along with $5.00 to cover all costs to:

IMPACT BOOKS, INC.
137 W. Jefferson
Kirkwood, MO 63122

NOTE: If you honestly cannot afford to pay for the tape, we will send it to you free of charge.

DELIVERANCE FROM FAT & EATING DISORDERS

❖ Why have so many so often failed to lose unwanted weight?

❖ Can weight gain sometimes truly be *unnatural?*

❖ Could Anorexia Nervosa which is basically suicide by starvation, have spiritual roots?

❖ Might Bulimia, compulsive eating and food addictions have a common basis?

❖ What is the "Little Girl Spirit," and what role does it play in Bulimia?

In addition to answering the above questions, more than 80 causes for overeating are disclosed. The author clearly shows that there are many unsuspected roots and sources for over-weight conditions. Most overweight people really have no idea as to why they overeat, and often live in continual condemnation for not having sufficient will power or self discipline to control their weight. Many either feel rejected, or that they are unattractive.   **$5.95**

Are you aware that demonic spirits can prevent childbirth...?

DELIVERANCE FROM CHILDLESSNESS

This book offers the first real hope for certain childless couples, be-cause for some, there is a spiritual rather than a physical block prevent-ing conception.

The testimonies included will build your faith as will the Scriptural truths revealed. You will also learn:

✿ HOW CURSES OF CHILDLESSNESS COME INTO BEING, AND HOW THEY MAY BE BROKEN.

✿ WAYS THAT SPIRITS OF INFERTILITY AND STERILITY ENTER, AND HOW TO CAST THEM OUT.

In the first year of publication eight women who had been told they were incapable of having children, advised us that they had *become pregnant after reading this book.*   **$5.95**